Pianism

Aiko Onishi

Originally published in Japanese under the title of:
APPROACH TO PIANISM
Copyright © 1996 by Zen-On Music Company Ltd.
All Rights Reserved
International Copyright Secured

Published in the United States by Anima Press

Preface

This book is the result of encouragement and prodding from numerous students I have taught here in the U.S. and abroad, who felt that the limited anthology on piano playing did not contain many of the subtleties which every student should learn.

I had the rare privilege and good fortune to study with three distinguished teachers-- Cecile Genhart, Frank Mannheimer and Dame Myra Hess, all of whom had studied with Tobias Matthay. Each had a different approach to teaching though they were most complementary. All three were unselfishly devoted to their students. After very successful careers both Cecile Genhart and Frank Mannheimer shunned publicity in their later lives and concentrated on teaching while Dame Myra Hess continued to enjoy a brilliant career as an international concert pianist.

Cecile Genhart was one of Edwin Fischer's favorite students. She was most analytical and meticulous. She taught me how to <u>listen to</u> and <u>feel</u> each note and gave me the solid foundation and confidence to develop on my own. Her vast knowledge was imparted in minute detail with discipline, generosity, and much love. She had an impeccable technique with a beautiful, luscious sound especially in the blending of harmonies. I cherish many wonderful memories of my six years of intensive study with her and of a lasting friendship.

Frank Mannheimer was a man of tremendous insight and wisdom who lived life to the full and eagerly anticipated the future. He must have had ESP as he could tell someone's past history after a brief meeting and knew who the caller was before picking up the telephone. This tremendous asset enabled him to maximize the individuality of each student in his teaching. He emphasized the spiritual qualities of the piece -- intense inner feeling, various moods and images. It was almost magical what he could do to make a piece come alive. I always came away from my lessons feeling transformed.

He inherited his relaxed and pure tone from Tobias Matthay. A most simple but elegant way of singing melodies made his Schubert playing memorable and his coloring in French music extraordinary. His friends and students were recipients of his kind generosity. It was he who, as my advisor and manager for many years, suggested that I meet Dame Myra Hess in London.

Dame Myra had already retired from the concert stage when I began studying with her but she continued to make music by teaching a few students. She had one student each day to play as many pieces as were prepared. My lessons began at eleven o'clock and lasted until three or three thirty when I had exhausted my repertoire for the session. I always felt extremely musical at her home, undoubtedly due to her enormously rich and grand conception. It was indeed a privilege to have been associated with such a great artist.

I thank my friends and students who have persisted in encouraging me to write this book and who have given me joy by allowing me to share my knowledge with them. My sincere thanks to Greg Anderson for his time and effort in creating the book cover and making the book available online. I am also grateful to Charlie Cramer who provided an original photo for the book cover and to Anne Hart for her assistance.

I hope that this little book will prove helpful to other students of the piano as well as a refresher for my students and friends.

Aiko Onishi
April 2009

Cécile Staub Genhart (1898-1983), born in Switzerland and received her early training from her father, Gottfried Staub, who was a well known concert pianist, who taught at Basel Conservatory and later at the Zurich Conservatory. Cécile Genhardt studied with Emile Frey at the Zurich Conservatory, Josef Pembauer in Munich, and Edwin Fischer in Berlin. After very successful tours in Europe, she came to the Eastman School of Music to teach and to concertize. She was a tremendously sensitive and beautiful pianist but she devoted her life to teaching, producing numerous accomplished pianists as well as international competition winners.

Frank Mannheimer (1896-1972) studied briefly in Berlin and Paris, but it was Tobias Matthay in London whom Mr. Mannheimer adored and stayed with as his assistant teacher at the Matthay School. He concertized and taught extensively both in Europe and in the U.S. During World War II, since he was unable to return to London, he began conducting master classes throughout the United States. Every summer he returned to Duluth, Minnesota where he taught for 30 years. Students/Artists of all ages from all over the world attended his classes.

Dame Myra Hess (1890-1965) started her studies with Tobias Matthay at the age of 12 at the Royal Academy of Music in London. She made a brilliant debut in London playing the Beethoven G Major Concerto with Sir Thomas Beecham. After this immediate success, she played with all of the major orchestras of the world. She made regular appearances in the U.S. and Canada from 1922. During World War II she established the immensely popular daily chamber concerts at the National Gallery and played in many of them herself. She was made a Dame of the British Empire in 1941.

About the Author

Aiko Onishi was born in Tokyo, Japan. She started learning the piano from her mother, Teiko, an accomplished pianist and a graduate of the New England Conservatory of Music. She later studied with Mr. Motinari Iguchi and Miss Aiko Iguchi, his sister.

Upon winning a Japan National Competition, she was invited to study at the Eastman School of Music with Madam Cécile Genhart, who gave her a real foundation as a pianist. After earning the B.M. with Distinction, Performer's Certificate, and Artist's diploma, she continued to study with Frank Mannheimer; with whom she coached on and off for the next sixteen years. During the winter of 1964-65, she had the great privilege of studying with Dame Myra Hess in London.

Aiko Onishi has concertized and given lectures in over 60 cities in the United States, and has played in all of the major cities in Japan. She was a professor for six years at the Toho School of Music in Japan and for twenty-one years at San Jose State University in California. As a teacher, Miss Onishi has produced many outstanding students, some of whom have won prizes at international competitions–including Leeds, Busoni, Casadesus, Kapell, Chopin, Munich, University of Maryland, and the Washington International Competition

TABLE OF CONTENTS

Chapter		Page
1	TONE PRODUCTION	1
	Tone Quality	3
2	PEDALING	12
	Various Characteristics of the Damper Pedal	13
	Various Uses of Pedaling	16
3	TECHNIQUE	26
	The Hand and Its Rotation	26
	Use of Rotation in Playing Scales	27
	Various Ways of Practicing Scales	28
	Arpeggio and Broken Chords	30
	Miscellaneous Techniques	31
	Fingering	47
4	MELODY AND HARMONY	53
	Regrouping	53
	Treatment of Melody	56
	Slurs	66
	Voicing and Coloring	69
	Harmony	73
5	SALIENT INTERPRETATIONAL EXPRESSIONS	79
	Some Musical Concepts	79
	Definition of Some Musical Terms	86
6	EXERCISES	89
	Stretching Exercises	89
	Correcting the Double-Jointed Thumb	92
	Strengthening the First Joints	94
	Exercises for Instant Key Release	95

Chapter		Page
7	RUDIMENTS OF LEARNING AND PERFORMING	97
	How to Learn a New Piece	97
	Memory	99
	Imagery	103
	Preparation for Performing	104
8	PEDAGOGY	107
	Playing Posture	107
	Hand Position	107
	Playing for the First Time	108
	Ear Training	109
	Transposition	111
	Reading	111
	First Lessons and Practicing	112
	Challenging Students	113
9	PIANISTIC ANALYSIS	114
	Chopin Nocturne	114
	Debussy Pedaling	116
	Ravel's Coloring	120
INDEX		123

Chapter 1

TONE PRODUCTION

Producing tone at the piano requires an understanding of the physical mechanism which makes the sound. Figure 1.1 shows the complex nature of the piano action with all of its numerous parts. While it is important to be aware of the workings of these individual components, one must also be aware of how they interact together. For example, once the hammer strikes the strings, it comes back to rest on the backcheck before falling back to its original position. When the hammer is resting on the backcheck--this is only for a moment--the key can be played again, which makes playing the repeated notes much easier.

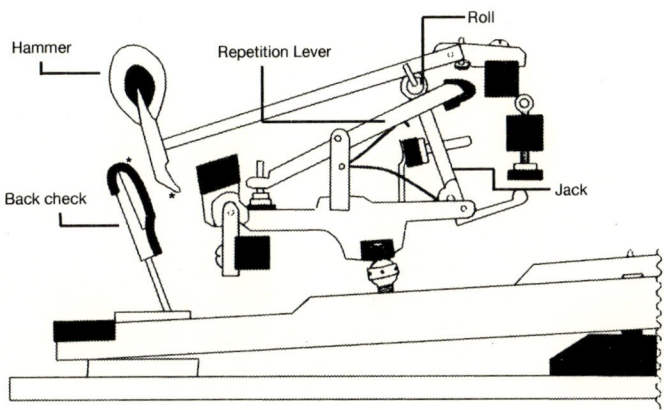

Figure 1.1. Piano mechanism.

Two points marked with * meet when the hammer rests on the backcheck before falling down.

Tone Spot.
Sound is produced at a place called the tone spot, time spot, or key spot (which piano tuners call after-touch). This point is where the key has moved through two-thirds of its path

to the bottom. The keybed (Fig. 1.2) has a springy touch so that the finger bounces up. Since the sound is already made at the tone spot in descending, one only needs to release the exertion at this spot rather than picking up the fingers after playing. The sound continues when the key is held at the tone spot. The pp tone should go down only to the tone spot since the speed of depression is slow. However, for virtually all other sounds, the fingers will descend into the keybed, though the intended physical action should be released at the tone spot.

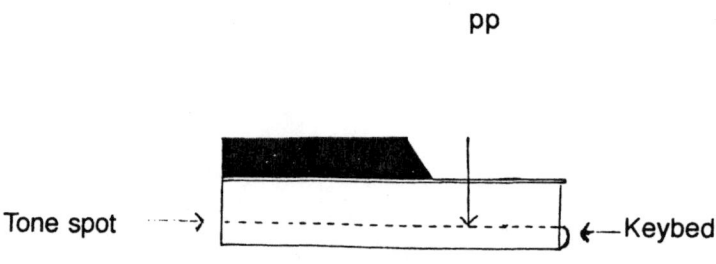

Fig. 1.2. Tone spot for pp on keybed.

The speed of the key descent determines the amount of sound obtained. Depressing a key with greater speed produces a louder sound and the opposite is also true. Speed is also the variable the performer employs in order to produce different tone colors. It must always be kept in mind that strings make the sound. To produce a soft pizzicato sound on a harp or any string instrument, one would use the very tip of a finger to touch the string and pluck lightly and quickly. For a slightly louder pizzicato, the string needs to be plucked more rapidly. Thus just the fingertip (first joint) movement is involved. To produce a loud, brilliant pizzicato sound, one would use more of the whole finger or even the whole hand to pluck the string. In contrast, a rich sonorous sound is produced by using the whole finger much more slowly and letting the string vibrate with slow but greater motion. The image of plucking a harp string can be very useful in approaching a piano key. If one touches the key in preparation, pre-listening to the tone one wishes, and plucks it at the tone spot, the sound produced is exactly what was intended. Always prepare mentally for each note.

Keybed

Holding the key down at the bottom after producing a sound, called key-bedding, is to be avoided at all times. There are two reasons for this. The tone is never beautiful because the maximum speed is not met at the tone spot but at the bottom of the key. Sound should be made and released when the speed is the greatest which should coincide with reaching the tone spot. Another reason is that the extra unnecessary force holding down the key makes the next move difficult, thus interfering with relaxation and the preparation of the next keys to be played. Needless to say, it is also hard on the hand and the arm.

Tone Quality

Colorless Tone

Colorless or white tone is produced by depressing the key straight down as slowly and as evenly as possible (see Fig. 1.2). This is the softest sound one can produce at the piano. Since it is dull and does not carry, this is used mainly for background sound or distant effect.

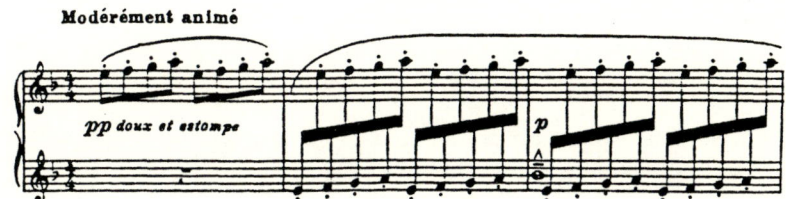

Example 1.1. Debussy, "La neige danse" from The Children's Corner

The sound can easily be demonstrated by placing a pencil against a key vertically and pushing on the pencil slowly and evenly. Colorless tone is also called dead or transparent.

Harmonious Tone

Music often calls for gentle, harmonious tone, which blends with other tones to make soft, luscious sounds as in chordal passages, arpeggiated harmonic figuration including Alberti Bass. For this, use a brushing touch. This sound is produced by depressing the key slowly just to the tone spot using a curved motion. The feeling is as though the key were being dusted with the ball of the finger. Do not hesitate to slide out using an inch or more on the key. In other words, the finger should be quite flat, stretched and loose on the key. The hand hangs from the wrist. Now play slowly and gently towards you from the wrist using individual fingers as little as possible. Suggestions of caressing a kitten or using the hand as a wet mop work well. The reason for brushing (sliding down to the tone spot) is to lengthen the distance between the surface of the key to the tone spot for better control.

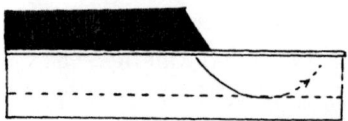

Figure 1.3. Brushing touch on keybed.

The dynamic level can be adjusted simply by making the key go down slowly to the tone spot for p, and a little deeper and faster for a fuller sound. However beautiful, this sound is used for background or harmonious sound exclusively.

Example 1.2. Beethoven Sonata Op. 27 #2 - First Movement

Example 1.3. Schumann: Fantasia Op. 17 - Third Movement

Singing Tone

The singing tone can be described as sympathetic, warm and clear, suitable for melody. Here one uses the fingertip, first joint, to mold, which means to go down on the key with accelerando using the ball of the finger similar to molding clay or hard bread dough. In preparation, the finger is not as flat as in the harmonious tone but is flat enough to play with the ball of the finger. A slight hand weight travels through to the tip of the finger as though placing a thumb tack. Therefore, the center of the hand should be placed behind each finger being played, holding the wrist in a somewhat higher position.

For Piano Singing Tone, molding starts about one-third before the tone spot is reached.

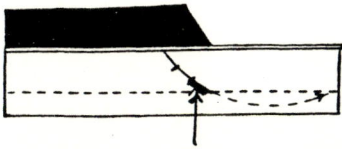

Figure 1.4. Piano singing tone.

For Forte Singing Tone, molding starts earlier resulting in faster descent though the point of release should always be at the tone spot as in every touch to secure the clear "ring" in tone.

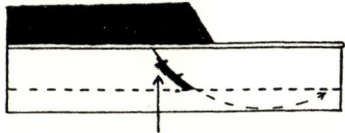

Figure 1.5. Forte singing tone.

Use of Weight

Because the hand weight is not enough for a rich resonant tone, one must resort to the use of the forearm or the whole arm. If the wrist is low, the weight will be held at the wrist and will not have the chance to travel through the hand. Whatever the weight being used, it must always be behind the finger being played and held higher than the joint(s) closest to the keys (gravity). In other words, when using hand weight, the wrist is raised. The use of forearm weight requires the elbow to move away from the body so that the elbow will be equal to or even higher than the wrist while the wrist still remains higher than the bridge. This allows the weight to travel down the forearm through the hand and fingers. The shoulder must always be low and loose. Now touch the key and mold the weight into it, using the first joint, while feeling the key descend. Without touching the key in preparation and molding its way down, the sound becomes harsh as in hitting. An analogy to this kind of tone production again can be made to depressing a thumb tack. One must feel the tack with the ball of the finger, aim, apply speed and weight vertically, first slowly and then accelerating until the tack is firmly in place, and relax as soon as it is in place. The more weight and acceleration used, the louder the sound that is produced.

Rich and Full Chordal Tone

Each note of a chord should be played as a rich singing tone since inner notes are often neglected. There is a vast difference in resonance with molding or without. Occasionally for the really big ff chords one can use the upper body, raising the shoulder a little and letting it down as one swings the whole arm weight into the keys, molding as much as possible.

Bell-like Tone

A light tone with clarity is produced with the nail-under touch. This means curving and fixing the first joint as much as possible so the tip of the fingernail touches the key with a high wrist. The sound is made by plucking the key as lightly and quickly as possible by wrist motion. The wrist must be loose enough to give a light kick (or pluck) with the firmly fixed fingertip. Since the fingernail slides more easily on the key than the fingertip, the speed of the key descent is much greater, resulting in clear, ringing tone. The amount of the sound can be varied from pp, barely touching the tone spot, to about mf going slightly deeper into the keys.

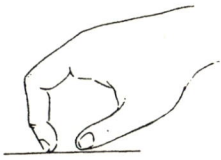

Figure 1.6. Nail-under touch.

Since the tone is of great clarity, it is most effectively used as the 'bell' effect often found in Debussy or 'glittering color' in Ravel's high notes.

Example 1.4. Debussy: "Reflets dans l'eau" from Images, Book I

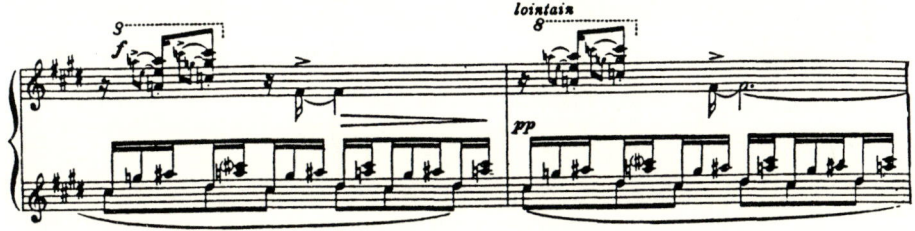

Example 1.5. Ravel: "Oiseaux tristes" from Miroirs.

Some melodies in the Classic or Romantic Periods can also be played successfully when great clarity without much tone is called for.

Example 1.6. Beethoven: Sonata Op. 110 - Third Movement.

For a group of fast notes, each finger lines up and plucks the key in one quick motion. "Scratching" often gets the right result. One can practice this on the table top to feel loose and get an even and quick "bullet" sound. The hand position is exactly the same as nail-under touch, also with a high wrist.

Example 1.7. Beethoven: Sonata Op. 2 #2 - Third Movement.

Bright Tone (single note or chord)
Instead of descending, it works best to bounce off the key as quickly as possible. Touch the key with firm fingertips and give a sharp bounce (kick) from the wrist, using the motion to move directly to the next position. This avoids hitting and results in a well-prepared bright tone.

Arm Vibration
This touch is used for detached melody notes or a consecutive bright tone on fast climactic passages. The wrist and the elbow must be held high to free the weight of the forearm (or whole arm) and the weight bounces from one finger to the next with an up and down motion. This cannot be done too quickly because of the individual motion called for, therefore only a few notes in succession can be produced.

Example 1.8. Chopin: Etude Op. 10 #9.

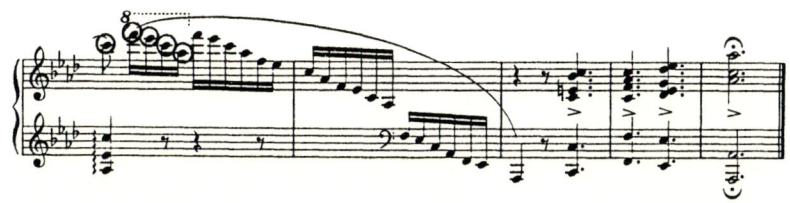

Example 1.9. Chopin: Ballade Op. 47.

Weight Transfer Legato

Legato is always very important in music. One can make a smooth and beautiful legato through the use of weight transfer which can best be described as sneaking. When one sneaks, one foot (finger) supports the body (hand) weight and the other foot (next finger) is placed silently on the floor (key). Then the weight is transferred gradually. In principle, the motion is the same as in playing slurs. For a two-note slur, one uses "down and up" motion; one weight to travel through two fingers. A finger goes down on the key, leans towards the next finger, which is already placed on the next key, and plays as the hand goes halfway up in release. The fingers hardly articulate, but the whole hand moves from the wrist, resembling the way an octopus moves its tentacles with complete looseness and smoothness using its suckers (ball of the fingers) to transfer the weight. Learn to add more notes and to move in either direction freely.

Double Legato (Overlapping)

Stylistically this technique is not suitable for use in Baroque or early Classic music, but is very often employed in Romantic and French music. Double legato is produced by delaying the release of the key until after a succeeding sound is made in order to blend the sounds for an instant. It is used successfully when intervals of the notes are wider and harmonious in melodic passages. Tremendous caution is required in passages that are non-harmonic and/or in a low register, since this can blur easily.

Example 1.10. Chopin: Etude Op. 25 #7.

Staccato

Never play the staccato without touching the key first, otherwise you will end up hitting, instead of playing. One would not think of hitting a harp string for fear of making a bad, harsh sound. Touch the key and pluck according to the tone quality desired as in pizzicato. Rather than bouncing straight up, bounce off to the next position to rest and prepare.

As mentioned earlier, release at the tone spot for the best tone quality. However, for a big sound as in forte melodic tone, rich chordal tone, and in forte arm vibration touch, one should aim to the bottom of the keys since the speed and the weight required are so great.

To summarize the correct approach for playing, mentally go through the following steps:
1. Think about the quality of the tone to be produced.
2. Relax and feel the surface of the keys before beginning the descent.
3. Move the first joint mentally while maintaining a floating (relaxed) arm.
   Feel the resistance of the keys during the descent to the tone spot.
4. Avoid key bedding by releasing the fingers as soon as the sound is made.
5. Listen to the tone produced, resting at the tone spots.

"Producing a tone is exactly like throwing a ball." (Cécile Genhart)
- a. One needs to know precisely what kind of ball, which direction and how far to throw. (Pre-listening).
- b. Preparation with a ball in the hand, all joints as loose as possible.
- c. Start accelerando so that the intended maximum speed is reached at the moment the ball leaves the hand. (The tone is aimed and produced at the tone spot.)
- d. Relax instantly. (Relax as soon as the tone is made.)
- e. The hand, though the ball has been released, still continues to follow through while the eye follows the ball to its destination. (Listen to the tone.)

Chapter 2

PEDALING

The three pedals on the piano, from left to right, are the Una Corda or Soft pedal, the Sostenuto pedal, and the Damper pedal

Figure 2.1. Una Corda, Sostenuto, and Damper pedals.

The Una Corda Pedal, often called the soft pedal, has evolved from shifting the entire action to the right so that the hammers play one string (una corda) per note instead of two strings in the earlier pianos. In the modern grand pianos, the hammers play two out of three strings, therefore the indication to release is tre corde. The mechanism in the upright piano for this pedal brings the action closer to the strings, thus decreasing the volume. One needs to be careful in using this pedal because the tone loses clarity on most grand pianos when applied.

The Sostenuto Pedal is used for sustaining one to several notes while playing other notes. The notes to be sustained must be held when the left foot depresses the middle pedal. Once the pedal catches these notes, they are sustained as long as the pedal is held down. The same notes can be played again without changing the pedal, however, the tone quality and volume of these notes cannot be controlled too well once engaged. It is very convenient to use on the f pedal point, but not appropriate for passages requiring sensitive tone qualities. The damper pedal can be used simultaneously with the sostenuto pedal without any restrictions.

Example 2.1. Bach-Busoni: Chaconne

The <u>Damper Pedal</u> is connected to the dampers which sit on the strings to dampen the sound (vibration) caused by the hammers. The dampers are larger in the lower register, smaller in the upper register, and lacking in the very high notes. When a key is played, the damper goes up, leaving the strings to vibrate freely. When the damper pedal is engaged, all of the dampers go up, letting all the strings vibrate in sympathy with the one which is being played.

Various Characteristics of the Damper Pedal

<u>The pedal enhances the tone quality</u>. As mentioned above, when the damper pedal is used, sympathetic vibration occurs among the rest of the strings. Thus the tone is much more sonorous. When playing single notes, especially in the high register, it is advisable to use the pedal to achieve good tone quality. When the first note or chord calls for resonant tone quality, the pedal should be engaged before the tone is produced to obtain all of the vibration possible. One can hear the distinct differences in tone quality by depressing the pedal before, together, or after playing the note.

Example 2.2. Beethoven's Concerto Op. 58 - First Movement

Example 2.3. Brahms's Intermezzo Op. 118 #6

<u>Control the amount by depth</u>. The depth of depression controls the amount of pedal being used. For example, keep playing staccato on one note while depressing the pedal very slowly to see when it starts to work. Normally the first one-eighth inch or so does nothing. Then it begins to work gradually and increases until the pedal is fully engaged when it reaches three-fourths of the way down. The amounts and depth vary greatly among individual instruments. A piano technician can adjust the depth as well as the resistance of the pedal.

Another significant characteristic is that the sound in the lower register is sustained considerably longer than the treble. It is easy to prove this by playing chords in two extreme registers and lifting the pedal very gradually, listening to the high tones disappear half way up while the bass sustains. If this does not happen, the pedal should be regulated.

<u>More pedal in high register, less in bass</u>. The lower notes sound louder with less clarity of pitch. Especially on modern pianos, they can easily become blurry. Therefore, one needs to carefully release the pedal while playing in the bass, whereas high notes can remain clearer, providing opportunities for longer pedaling.

<u>Danger of pedaling small intervals</u>. Even in the higher register, short intervals, especially half steps, are the most dangerous in pedaling. One normally changes pedals according to the harmony. However, when the melody moves stepwise for example, it is often necessary to change either completely or half way (half-pedaling) on each note even in the same harmonic accompaniment. On the other hand, when the music is written in pentatonic or whole tone scale, one can take much longer pedaling, as in Debussy. (Refer to Pedaling in Debussy, Chapter 9.)

Use of long pedal on repeated notes. The pedal exposes the note(s) when taken. On repeated notes or chords, release the pedal only when emphasis is needed, but not when the sound should be continuous. On the contrary, the pedal is effectively taken on beats on syncopation to give steadier rhythm.

Example 2.4. Mozart: Sonata K. 311 - First Movement

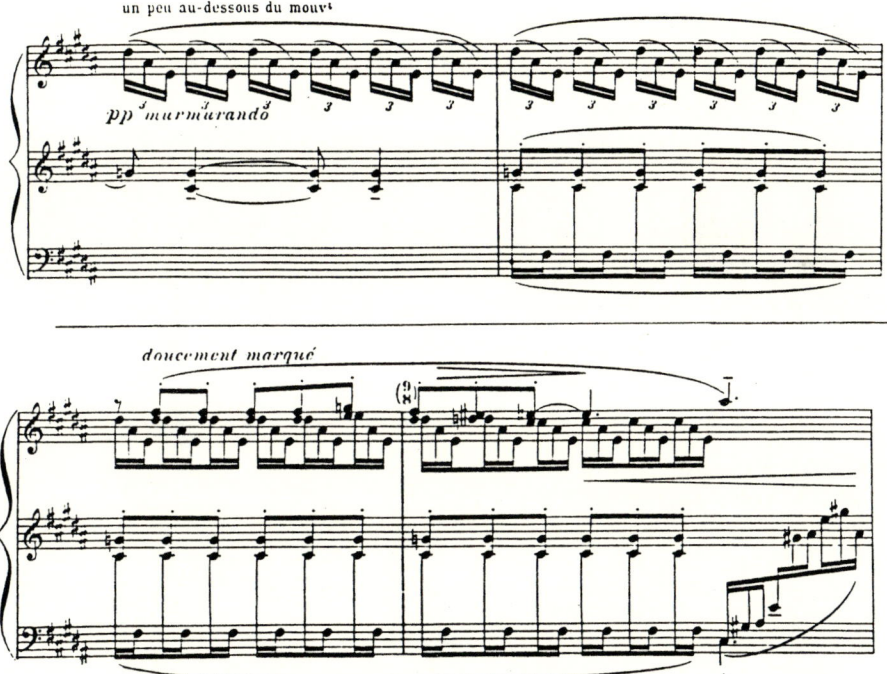

Example 2.5. Debussy: Prelude "Ondine"

Various Uses of Pedaling

Syncopated Pedal (Legato or Sustaining Pedal)
The most common use of the pedal is to sustain one note/chord to the next. The foot comes up when the sound is made, not before. In other words, the foot action follows the finger action. The base of the big toe should always be in contact with the surface of the pedal, requiring minimum motion and avoiding any tapping sound. To release it, simply release the pressure so that the pedal brings the foot back up.

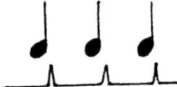

Figure 2.2.

Overlapping Pedal
This form of pedaling blends the sound. It is done by bringing the foot up slowly after the notes are played so that the mixture of both sounds can be heard for an instant (see the grey area in Figure 2.3).

Figure 2.3.

This is not suitable for Baroque or the early Classic literature. It is commonly used to blend harmonic sound in the Romantic works.

Example 2.6. Brahms: Intermezzo

Half-Pedal (a very convenient and versatile pedal)

As mentioned earlier, when the pedal is raised halfway from the bottom, the bass is still sustained but the treble is cleared. The amount of clearing depends entirely on the sound desired. Sometimes the pedal may come up only one-fourth or one-third from the bottom but they are all categorized as half-pedaling.

Much of the 'magical beauty' in playing is done by half-pedaling. Chopin in particular was known to have used it all of the time ("Musical Interpretation" by Tobias Matthay, p. 89). Some other composers, for instance Debussy, must have known the use of half-pedaling because there are many passages calling for sustaining bass and clearing treble since European pianos in their time did not have the Sostenuto Pedal.

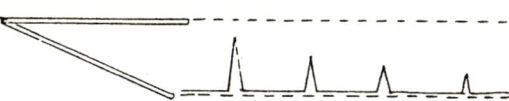

Figure 2.4. Side view of various depths of depression

Shown below is an example Beethoven used to create the effect he desired with the long pedal indication. It is indeed beautiful to keep the long pedal as he indicated on the Fortepiano of his period, giving just enough shimmering blend to create an ethereal, mysterious quality. However, on our modern pianos, the sound sustains too long, resulting in a blur. Half-pedaling is just the answer to keep the blending tone thin enough to create the desired effect.

Example 2.7. Beethoven: Sonata Op. 31 #2 - First Movement

Another use of half-pedaling can be seen in thinning the sound inconspicuously to avoid thickness, as in Debussy's "La Cathédrale engloutie."

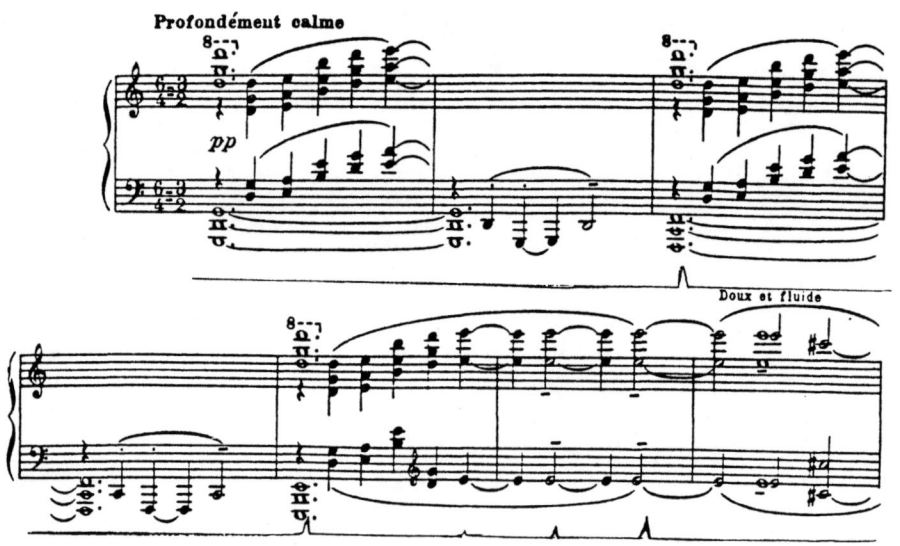

Example 2.8. Debussy: Prelude, "La Cathédrale engloutie"

The half pedal is used so commonly that it will be difficult to find a page of lyrical pieces from the Romantic or French Impressionistic literature which does not require it.

A Chopin Nocturne offers a good example of using the combination of one quarter pedaling to three quarters pedaling.

Example 2.9. Chopin: Nocturne Op. 62 #2

The opening of the Barcarolle is another excellent way of gradual one quarter to three quarters pedaling, keeping the bass to the end.

Example 2.10. Chopin: Barcarolle Op. 60

Half-Damping Pedal
The pedal is depressed halfway and held there to create the effect of the passge being somewhat pedaled. The level of the pedal can be varied to obtain the exact sound needed.

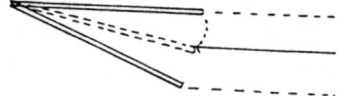

Figure 2.6. Side view of pedal for half-damping

It requires very keen listening and sensitive application of pressure. Light half-damping is most always used in long trills to avoid dryness, or in Alberti Bass passages in slow movements so they sound harmonious enough. This should be applied very subtly so it will not be blurry.

Example 2.11. Mozart: Sonata K. 333 - First Movement

Half-damping is also commonly used in French music for blending sound.

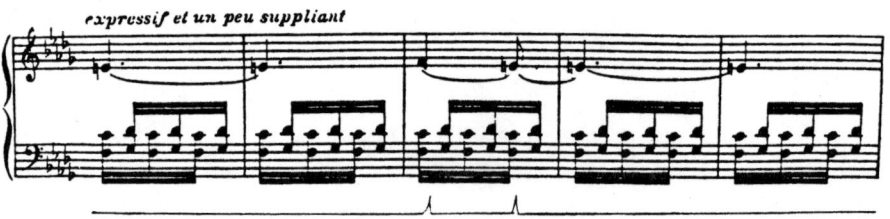

Example 2.12. Debussy: Prelude, "La sérénade interrompué"

Finger Pedal

This technique is mainly used in Alberti Bass or arpeggiated accompaniment passages where one does not want to use pedal due to the melodic figuration. Instead of pedaling, hold the keys with the fingers as though pedaled but without using the pedal. This form of pedaling yields a harmonious sound in the accompaniment without blurring the melodic line.

Example 2.13. Beethoven: Sonata Op. 14 #2 - First Movement

Fluttering Pedal (Trill or Shaking Pedal)

As the name indicates, the foot goes up and down rapidly like a finger trill while using only one-fourth to one-third of the upper portion of the pedal.

Figure 2.7. Fluttering pedal

Normally, this pedal is used in fast scale passages. It is as though pedaling lightly on each note thus producing a more resonant sound without being too dry or too blurry.

Example 2.14. Beethoven: Piano Concerto No. IV, Op. 58

This technique also can be used with long chords for a beautifully shimmering sound when molto diminuendo is desired.

Example 2.15. Beethoven: Sonata Op. 109 - Third Movement

Another use of the fluttering pedal is to diminish the f tone as quickly as possible for an fp effect. The usual syncopated pedal will not only sustain too much sound, but will make the following chord less clear as in the following example.

Example 2.16. Beethoven: Sonata Op. 13 - First Movement

Crescendo Pedal

This is created by starting to flutter close to the surface and going down gradually deeper as the passage continues.

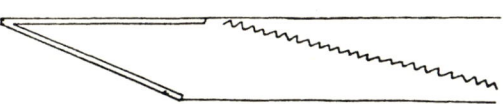

Figure 2.8. Side view of crescendo pedal

This normally accompanies ascending crescendo passages to enhance the crescendo sound without getting too blurry in the lower register.

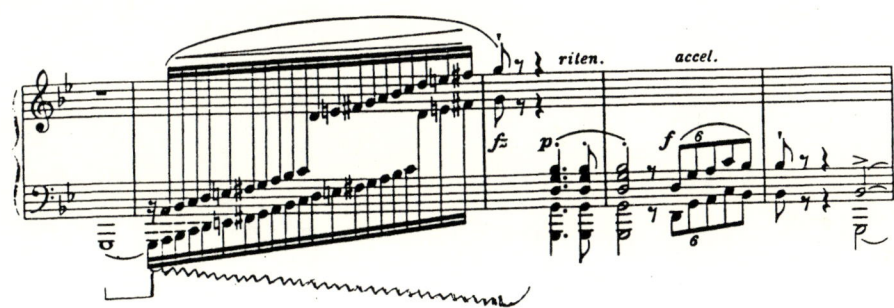

Example 2.17. Chopin: Ballade Op. 23

<u>Diminuendo Pedal</u> is the reverse of the crescendo pedal. The fluttering starts halfway down and gradually comes up to accompany fast descending diminuendo passages.

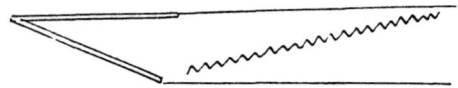

Figure 2.9. Side view of diminuendo pedal

An example of this is seen in Chopin's Etude Op. 10 #12.

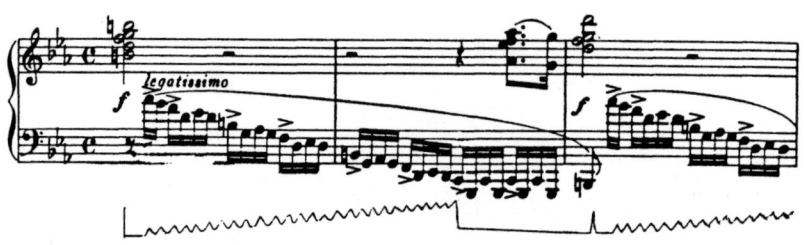

Example 2.18. Chopin: Etude Op. 10 #12

Staccato Pedal

This is the only time the foot and finger simultaneously move down and up to make the sound more resonant. The staccato pedal can be used most effectively to replace an accent. The pedal must not lengthen the duration of the staccato.

Example 2.19. Brahms: Sonata Op. 5 - Third Movement

All of the techniques discussed above are frequently used in various combinations.

Except for some composers as Bartok, Debussy, and Beethoven, who were particular in indicating long pedal markings, it is not recommended to follow the printed pedal markings too literally because much editing has been done by the editors rather than the composers. Even when the markings are done by the composers, some compromise is often necessary to adjust to the sound of modern pianos and acoustics. The ear must be trained and must always be fostered and developed. Critical listening should be the guide for sensitive pedaling at all times.

Chapter 3

TECHNIQUE

The Hand and Its Rotation

There are two big bones in the forearm. Dropping the whole arm down will put the thumb in front with the fifth finger towards the back. In this position these two bones hang parallel. When one places the hand on the lap without twisting these bones, the hand rests on the fifth finger side, the thumb on the top. However, when the hand is placed on the keyboard, one has to twist the hand towards the thumb, causing the bones to cross. Since our natural position is to have the thumb side higher, it is important that one does not rotate too much towards the thumb. Also, if the hand is cut in half, the thumbside is heavier, which contributes to the heavy or sticky thumb. Tilting back towards the fifth finger in some fast passages often solves the problem.

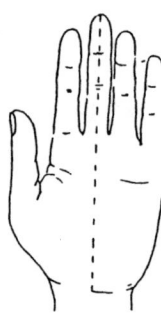

Figure 3.1. Heavy and light side of the hand.

The thumb and the fifth finger are shorter. Lateral rotation from the wrist to place the hand behind each finger which is being played compensates this shortcoming. Tobias Matthay says that there is no weak finger if it is supported by the hand behind the finger (<u>Visible and Invisible Pianoforte Technique</u> by T. Matthay).

Normally, if the fingertips are nicely curved and placed on adjacent white keys, the hand position on the keyboard can be described as an arch.

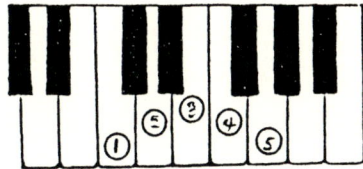

Figure 3.2. Correct fingertip position for 5 notes to be played.

Use of Rotation in Playing Scales

When playing scales, the fingers move into a position closer to a diagonal line.

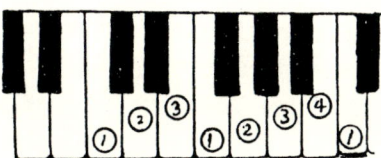

Figure 3.3. Correct fingertip position for scales.

When playing an ascending scale with the right hand or a descending one with the left, the wrist should be rotated as soon as the thumb finishes playing so that the wrist and the arm will be in a straight line with the second finger. The thumb should hang down if relaxed. Continue to rotate for the third finger and raise the wrist slightly so that the thumb hangs almost at the edge of the next key to be played. Play the thumb as a finger from the second joint--in other words, do not let the hand drop with the thumb. This will not only change the tone quality and volume, but will hinder fast playing. Avoid crossed fingers which tighten the hand. Fingers 3 and 1 should play in a line. The rotation is done by the wrist. The elbow should be free to follow but not to lead.

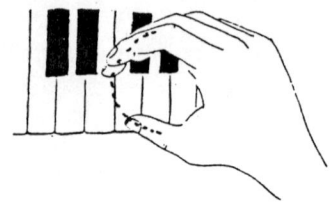 

Figure 3.4.   (a) Correct position   (b) Wrong position (crossed thumb)

When playing a descending scale with the right hand and ascending scale with the left hand, keep the wrist high and use the thumb as a pivot so that the third or fourth finger can rotate as a compass.

Various Ways of Practicing Scales

In learning scales, it helps to block 123 and 1234 as chords and play them up and down the keyboard. One not only learns placement of the thumbs, but the placement of each finger tip on the keyboard where it ought to be played. In other words, if the fourth finger falls on a black key, the third finger will be placed close to the black key, etc. If the third finger also plays a black key, then the whole hand position will be "in" (closer to the fall board) to avoid a jerky motion.

When scales are played rapidly, there will be less rotation, but it makes it much easier and the scales will sound smoother to have the freedom of the wrist rotation. The elbow always follows the wrist. Practice with exaggerated motion at first and then let the fingers do what they feel most naturally.

Scales can be practiced in many ways.
   1. Play one hand legato, the other staccato.
   2. Play one hand f, the other p.
   3. Play one hand in dotted rhythm, the other hand evenly.
   4. Play 2 against 3.
   5. Play tow kinds of scales simultaneously, i.e., R.H. Ab Major and L.H. E major. Especially good in contra motion.
   6. Use C major fingerings for the rest of the scales.

Double Third Scale

When playing double thirds, the upper notes in the right hand are normally more important as melody. Practice the upper line alone with the correct fingering as legato as possible. Add lower notes staccato and pianissimo. This exercise enables one to rely on the upper line, keeping the lower notes from getting heavy thus interfering with the melody.

Often it helps to tilt the hand towards the direction of the scale. In the very fast tempo, the feel of non legato makes the playing clearer and easier, rather than trying to play too legato. Reverse the process for the left hand.

Chromatic Scale

Keep a slightly higher wrist for the chromatic scale playing so that the thumb, which plays six white keys out of eight, hangs, rather than having to move up and down all the time.

Figure 3.5.

The thumb and fingers should form a horseshoe, with the thumb playing close to the edge of the white keys as the other fingers do on the black keys. The thumb has the tendency to become heavy carrying the hand weight, if not careful.

There are three different fingerings as follows. The right hand ascending, starting from D.

1. 1 3 1 2 3 1 3 1 3 1 2 3 1, etc.
2. 1 3(2) 1 2 3 1 2 3 4 1 2 3 1, etc.
3. 1 2 3 1 2 3 4 1 2 3 1 2 3 4 1 2 3 1 2 3 4 1 2 3 1

The left hand descending will be the exact reverse.

For brilliant passages 1 is recommended. For smoother, much faster playing, 2 will be easier. The hardest but the fastest is 3. This is seldom used for the reason one may get confused since it takes two octaves to complete the cycle. If used, be sure to know where the thumb falls. One should invent one's own fingering--the combination of 123 and 1234 according to each passage in the music.

Whole Tone Scale

Pianistically there are only two kinds of whole tone scales, one starting on C, playing three white keys and three black keys. The other starts on B, playing two black keys and four white keys. Fingering for the whole tone scale is as follows:

R.H. ascending	Starting on B	Rh 123123123
		Lh 132132132
	Starting on C	Rh 121234121234
		Lh 121432121432

Reverse the pattern for descending scales.

To practice, play different whole tone scales in each hand simultaneously (e.g., the right hand starting on E and the left hand starting on C#, etc).

Arpeggio and Broken Chords

Arpeggio Practicing

As in playing scales, the same rotation is applied, however, the rotation is greater since the intervals are much wider. Getting into and out from the thumb needs to be practiced with a loose wrist. There should be no reason for a bumpy or even disconnected sound if the wrist is loose enough to rotate. Regrouping notes in various combinations works best for practicing for the smooth connection (please refer to "Regrouping" found later in Chapter 4). For example, practice 3 1 2, R.H. (G C E in C major) back and forth, then add more notes as 2 3 1 2 or 3 1 2 3. This is an excellent wrist exercise. Or play as many notes as possible as a chord according to the fingerings. The hand/fingers learn the distance of each interval this way.

Example 3.1. Blocking and regrouping in 3 ways. Chopin Etude, Op. 10 #1.

Number 1 blocks the C and E, Number 2 blocks the fourth, G and C and Number 3 blocks G C E. In practicing, play each note with good articulation and rotation either single notes or blocked making it as melodic as possible.

Another example of practicing the awkward position change is found below.

Example 3.2. Chopin Etude, Op. 25, #11.

Practice playing 52 together, then 524 together, or 4-1 524 blocked, then arpeggiated for the nicer connection. Whatever feels easy does not need attention. Concentrate on the groupings which feel awkward. Once a small group feels comfortable, increase the number of notes on both sides of the troublesome spot. Also, add another group until several are completed in a row.

When working on passages with broken arpeggios wrist rotation is done to make up for the short fingers, 1 and 5. The wrist should lead the fingers towards the direction, but always use the finger tips to play each note mentally with care. Never dissociate technique from musicality.

Miscellaneous Techniques

<u>The Turn</u>

Try playing all notes of the turn simultaneously with the correct fingering. (Let us try 34321.) By blocking the notes in this manner, the wrist is automatically raised and the elbow moves out away from the body unless the thumb or second finger falls on a black note. The fingers should outline a diamond shape when placed on the keys. Keep this position while the turn is executed; the wrist should rotate so that it draws a little circle every time the turn is played. Always sing each note as melodiously as possible, often requiring crescendo to the following principal note on the beat.

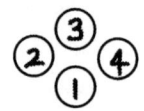

Figure 3.6. Position of each finger for the turn.

Combination of Trill and Turn

In general, the last two or three notes leading to the beat are the most beautiful. It is a good idea to practice backwards, e.g., D, E and F first, adding E to D E F, then another note F to E D E F, etc., finally to F E F E D E F. In this way, one learns to start softly relaxed and do the crescendo to the final F.

Example 3.3. Bach, "Courante" from Partita #1.

Trill

There are roughly two kinds of trill playing, articulated trill and shaking trill. The articulated trill is more often used in Baroque to the early Classic periods and whenever brilliant trills are called for. The shaking trill is faster, more harmonious and can be played much softer. Long trills found in the Romantic or French Impressionistic periods are often done as shaking trills to keep them in the background. The fingers are lightly fixed and the whole hand is shaken sideways from the wrist. Technically, if one can play the articulated trill well, playing the shaking trill should be easy.

For the articulated trill, the fingers play each note with clarity, which requires firm fingertips to achieve articulation. The following exercises are recommended:

1. Take two notes and play them quickly, the first one as a grace note, short and bright, and rest on the second note with an accent (12, 12, 12 - 21, 21, or 23, 23, 23 - 32, 32, 32, etc.).
2. Play triplets (e.g., 121, 212, 121, etc.) as crisply and quickly as possible ending on the third note also with an accent and rest.
3. Keep adding a note until a dozen or so notes become easy to play.

It is important that the wrist is always loose and the group of notes (2-, 3-, 4-, or 5-note pattern) is tossed off as one motion. Also, make certain that no weight from the hand or the arm creeps in. Notes must sound clearly and quickly. If one finger feels weak or a note is duller in sound, fix the hand position towards the dull sound. This usually solves the problem. If it doesn't, the weaker finger needs more work on rapid repetition. (A trill is simply repeated notes alternated between two fingers.) In this case, hold lightly onto the better finger and practice repeated notes with the weaker finger, start with two quick repeated notes and add a note as it gets easier. (Again there should be no tension and no weight.)

These exercises should be done not only using the adjacent fingers, i.e., 1 and 2, 2 and 3, etc. but 1 and 3, 2 and 4, 3 and 5. Whatever pairs of fingers are being used, one must be careful to have a loose wrist right behind them whenever possible. This requires some rotation for 12 13 towards the body and 35, 45 away from the body.

Another fingering is 1 3 2 3 1 3 2 3. This is less tiring and is suitable for long trills, though it is not as bright nor as fast as others.

One other exercise is to start f marcato in slow tempo and make accelerando with diminuendo until one cannot go any faster.

Since trill work requires the strenuous use of the same tendons, it must be practiced daily with care. One should not work too long at a time, especially using 3, 4 and 5 to avoid any injury.

<u>Double Trill</u>

Focus on one inner single trill on D# and C# rather than a set of two trills, as circled in the following examples. Thinking of a single trill frees one mentally and physically which results in achieving a better legato and sonorous sound. Practice a single trill in circles alone at first and add the upper note (E) to the trill. Add the lower note (B) without the E. If either one feels comfortable, then add both notes.

Example 3.4. Chopin Etude, Op. 25 #6.

The same applies to similar passages.

Example 3.5. Chopin Etude, Op. 25 #6.

Here again, thinking of the inner descending thirds makes the passage easier and more melodious.

False Trill

While trilling, there are other notes to be played simultaneously, as in the following example. Instead of keeping the trill going, the thumb notes are skipped while playing the upper notes. It will be not only considerably easier, but the texture becomes clearer. This is called *false trill* and is highly recommended in most cases.

Example 3.6. (a) Beethoven Sonata, Op. 109, 3rd movement.

(b) False trill execution.

Other Double Notes

When large and small intervals are combined in rapid tempo, play the small interval almost as nail under touch with a high, loose wrist and slide out towards the body. For large intervals, slide in towards the fallboard with firm first joints. The fingers should never lose contact with the keyboard. The wrist goes up with small intervals and down with large ones to create a rocking motion. This is the only time when an "in and out" motion is recommended on the keyboard. The major difficulty in playing these intervals is that the release is not quick enough. There is no molding into the keys. Rather, bounce off instantly and use the rebound to slide in and out. This is the only way to obtain a smooth, harmonious legato sound. When played with articulated fingers without the rocking mostion, it will sound notey in comparison. The motion required may take some time to feel comfortable.

Example 3.7. Chopin Etude, Op. 10 #7

Fast Repeated Notes

Let us take repeated notes to be played with the fingering 4 3 2 1 4 3 2 1. Instead of playing in the normal position, use the fingertips to play on the edge of the keys with a low wrist as shown in the example below. Use of the edge of the keys makes the fingers get off the keys instantly rather than having to pick them up. Thus the keys rebound more quickly, enabling the next finger to play right away. The fingers should line up vertically before playing, 4 on the key, 3 next and 2 at the top. Then, in one rapid motion, they fall straight down on the key. The thumb follows suit by moving in a quick downward motion off the edge of the key at an angle, releasing immediately.

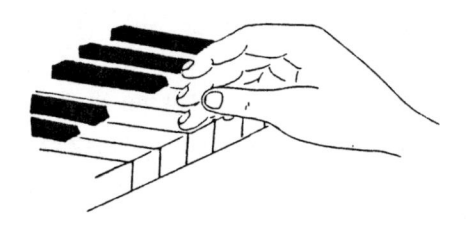

Figure 3.7. Hand position for repeated notes.

The hand ends up in a sweep. Let the fingers bounce on the keys rather than trying to control each finger. Keep the hand loose.

The common fault in repeated note passages is that they get too soft on ending, with dull thumb tone. To alleviate this problem, practice the passage with a crescendo to the thumb while giving the thumb a slight accent. Another important practice technique is to work on all possible combinations of regrouping to ensure a smooth connection, e.g., 3214, 2143, etc.

Succession of Staccato Chords

Touch the keys in preparation and bounce off to the next chords in a straight line close to the keyboard, avoiding any motion in the air. If the hand is not prepared ahead of time on the keys, it can result in hitting thus producing an undesirable tone.

In practicing, count 4 to each beat, 1 to play and bounce off to the next position on 2; then rest and prepare on 3 and 4.

Example 3.8. Chopin Ballade, Op. 52.

Doorknob Rotation

The doorknob rotation is a half-circle motion, clockwise or counterclockwise as used in turning a doorknob. This rotation is used when every other note needs to be brought out as in the following example.

Example 3.9. Beethoven Concerto, Op. 15, first movement.

To practice this rotation, hold the thumb lightly at the tone spot without making any sound. Play each note of the upper notes in succession individually with bounce. The first joint of fingers 2 through 5 must be fixed and the fingers bounce off the key with a quick motion in preparation for the next, producing a clear ringing tone. After this exercise feels comfortable, play the upper notes forte and the lower notes piano, using the same motion. The thumb should always be in contact with the key. Make sure the wrist and arm are completely loose. The first joints need to be firm on the upper notes for clarity.

Skips

It is difficult to gauge exactly how far to reach for intervals larger than the octave. Normally, coming up to the left-hand thumb is not a problem but going down (or up with the right hand) can be risky. To ensure precision and security, one can place the thumb an octave above the low note to shorten the skip by an octave.

Example 3.10. Chopin Waltz, Op. 64 #2.

1. Practice going down to the thumb from the previous chord as quickly as possible. Feel the key but do not play.
2. Do the same as above, only play the previous chord and the thumb as even eighth notes and add the bass (5). Perhaps write out the exercise.
3. Do the same as No. 2, keeping the thumb as a silent guide.
4. Practice the above without watching the hand.
5. Practice faster than a tempo.

If played this way, the skips cease to exist, but become a replacement of the thumb a step below or sixth below as in the above example. For skips, be sure to have loose joints, especially the shoulder. Any tension will cause rigidness and inaccuracy. The placement of the thumb keeps the hand weight from dropping on the bass notes. Any skips need to be placed with two motions to ensure the desired tone quality: (1) to get there, and (2) to play.

Balancing Oneself at the Piano

Unless one is a good-sized person having enough hand and arm weight to drop, it is easier to sit using only one-half of the piano bench, so that one can shift the body to balance using one's feet. One should always be in front of the register which is to be played ahead of time, if it is at all possible.

Shoulder Preparation

When both hands skip up and down covering a wide range of registers, the body needs to be there ahead of time. In other words, before one plays a chord preceding the skip, the body needs to move towards the direction of the next chord with the eyes focused on the notes looking over the shoulder. In this manner the shoulder will be naturally lowered and relaxed. By the time the hands get to the chord (always directly across the keyboard since a straight line is the shortest distance between two points), the body is already in front of the chord to be played.

Octaves

Fast Octave Passages. There are basically two ways to play rapid octave passages. Both require firm, but not tense fingertips.

For a lighter sound, fix the fingers in octave position and shake from the wrist, staying close to the keys. The wrist position is normally lower. However, when the passage is tiring, a gradual change of the wrist position can relieve the tension. To achieve a bigger tone, though the position will be more tiring, lightly fix the fingertips, hand and wrist, and use the elbow as a hinge.

Tensing can be psychological. A pianist could not get through playing the Erlkönig. In desperation, she squeezed her knees together as tightly as possible. The hand became free.

Short Repeated Octaves. For two or three fast repetitions, drop the weight on the first octave, regardless of the beat, and let it bounce off to the next as though throwing a stone to hop. If one aims to the last octave, the hand tightens up.

Example 3.11. Chopin Sonata, Op. 58, second movement.

Voicing of Octaves. It is seldom that one plays both notes of the octave alike. Generally, for the right hand, the top is favored for clarity, the bottom for the left hand for the bass melody. However, there are a number of exceptions.
1. When the bass is too low so as to become blurry.
2. The middle register (for either hand) gives better color to the texture.
3. The right- and left-hand thumbs share the melody line, as in the following example.

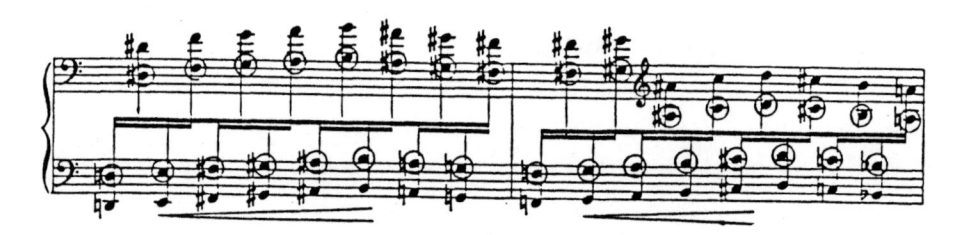

Example 3.12. Liszt, Hungarian Rhapsody #15.

Both thumbs should be played legato for the nice melodic line.

Octave Legato. Hold the wrist higher, but completely loose. Let the fingers hang from the wrist. Place the hand from one octave to the next as in flapping or dragging, using the brushing touch. The looser the hand, the easier to slide. For the nice tone, let the ball of the fingers give a little. Never rely on the pedal to connect the tone, instead learn to do the finger legato as much as possible. The tone is entirely different. Practice just the outer line (without the thumb) for the mellow, smooth tone and later add the pp thumb. One might practice playing each line with each hand (octaves with both hands), and figure out the tone quality, balance and inflection. Then practice with one hand to attain the same.

When connecting the top line is impossible, connect the top to the lower note or the lower to the top, rather than breaking the line, as in the following example.

Example 3.13. Beethoven Sonata, Op. 10 #1, first movement.

For the fast legato, do not try to connect each octave, instead detach them evenly. In any case, be sure to have all joints loose and play using the fingertips for nice tone.

Playing f and p Simultaneously

There are many occasions when a melody note is to be brought out and another note or notes to be played softer in the same hand. Hold the wrist high and drop the hand behind the finger on the f note to be played. Without releasing the exertion (this is the only time one should not release after the sound is made), play the other note(s) pp without moving the hand. Feel the sensation of this position--the first finger playing f sticking deeply into the key and the p finger(s) barely touching the tone spot. Repeat the above exercise for a few times, memorizing the hand position, then play them together.

If not successful, go back to the first exercise until it becomes so comfortable that one can produce f and pp any time. Do the same on the next set and learn how the hand should move from one position to the next.

In fugal playing, often the thumb note needs to be brought out. Tilt the hand towards the thumb so that the hand feels as though it is standing on the thumb. Mold with the thumb to avoid unprepared tone. As mentioned earlier, the hand is always tilted toward the f finger as much as possible in order to use the weight of the hand rather than the force.

Example 3.14. Bach, Fugue in Ab major from W.T.C., Vol. 1.

Organ Thumb

For legato playing from white key to the adjacent white key, but only in slow tempo, the organ thumb comes in handy. Play a note with a very low wrist at the edge of a key. Stick the thumb tip up to catch the corner of the next key and slide over (as a worm).

Figure 3.8. (a) Organ thumb as seen from above. (b) As seen from the side.

Playing pp Chords

Difficulty in playing pp is normally caused by tension somewhere in a joint. Find out where the tension is and let go or try shaking the hands just before playing in order to loosen up. (This should not be too visible to the audience.) Another way which works especially well for playing chords is to hold the hand in position, touch the keys and let the weight of the hand drop (collapse) gently onto the keys as though sinking into a cushion. There is no hand or finger motion involved. It is the releasing of the hand weight.

Preparation for the First Chords

When the first chords/notes are very beautiful, one tends to feel up-tight before playing, as in the opening of the Beethoven Fourth Concerto. Rest both hands on the lap. When the mood gets set and the tone is prepared in one's mind, pick up the hands and play right away before tightening up. When one places the hands on the keys in preparation, it is very easy for some tension to creep in.

Karate Chop

For ff on a single white note in low bass, line the fingers straight up sideways as 54321. Using a flexible hand and wrist, drop the whole hand weight on 5 into the key from wrist or even from the elbow joint. It is similar to a karate chop, only one needs to be very loose and in contact with the keys for good sonority. Never hit away from the key which could break the strings.

Flat Finger Tips for Black Keys

In playing the black keys which are tall and narrow, it is much easier and safer to play them with the ball of the fingers, since they are less likely to slip off the keys. The fingers can be completely straight if comfortable.

Playing ff on Black Notes in Bass

For a single black note place the finger straight from the bridge, using as a unit. One can support the finger with the thumb or other fingers for stability (e.g., 3 supported by 2 or 2 and 1). For double notes (as 3rd to 5th or 6th), make an arch with 1 and 3 or 1 and 3 and 4 together with the flattest finger tips. The wrist and the bridge should be fixed very high to take all of the weight dropped from the whole arm.

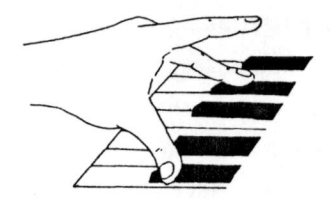

Figure 3.9.

Playing White Notes between Black Keys

It is common sense to avoid using 1 or 5 on black keys. Yet there are some passages where these fingers have to play the black keys. In these cases, play simultaneously as many notes as can be played as a chord including the thumb on the black key, as in the following example, and see where each finger places itself.

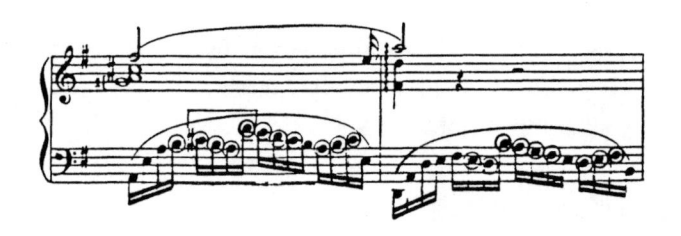

Example 3.15. Chopin Prelude, Op. 28, #3.

Rather than playing the circle BC#BA, etc. in the regular position, play the white keys well into the black keys, close to the fallboard in preparation for the thumb on F#, if the fingers are narrow enough to fit between the black keys. Play the passage in the position as one would play them together as a chord. In this way one can avoid a jerky in and out motion.

Playing Different Numbers of Notes Together

Often one needs to play 2 against 3, 3 against 4, 4 against 7, 6 against 10, etc. When introduced while one is very young, it is no problem at all. Yet for some, it can become very difficult to play them and make music at the same time.

Never think how the hands are to fit together. Never count them up and divide them evenly since music is not strictly mathematical. When melody is sung, there are subtle rubatos, hesitations and rit everywhere. However, the most simple--2 against 3--can be practiced as:

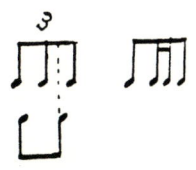

Figure 3.10. Sing along in rhythm "not dif-fic-ult"

Yet if the triplets are sung as a part of a melodic line, they are likely to have rubato. The same goes for any group of notes. Long passages may suggest more than one rubato. For this reason, a mathematical approach is not recommended.

In practicing 3 x 4 as an example, the best way to master it will be to learn each hand separately feeling strong beats. Then keeping the strong beat, alternate hands. In other words, play the R.H. in 3 and on the next beat take over with the L.H in 4. Repeat this until it feels very natural and then switch hands. Then put the hands together in short segments. For younger students, the teacher can play one hand while the student plays the other. The use of a metronome comes in handy here. The trick is never to figure out how the notes fall together, but depend on the feel of the hands. If one hand has the tendency to become uneven, play the hand f while playing the other hand p, so that one can hear the troublesome hand better.

Glissando

Relax and glide as loosely as possible. It helps to tilt one's hand as much as possible towards the direction, so that the keys to be played next are almost lowered in advance.

For a softer glissando on white notes, it is easier with 34 together in ascending passages (R.H.). Use the thumb with a light support with 2 or 3 for descending passages.

For a brilliant glissando, the thumb seems to take much more strength. For both directions support the thumb with 2 and 3; tilt the wrist towards the direction as low as possible. One can practice with a bandage on the finger to avoid scraping the skin until one learns the trick of relaxation. Beethoven among other composers wrote some octave glissandi--e.g., the Waldstein Sonata and the First Concerto. The fortepiano in his period had such light action so it was very easy to manage. On modern pianos, one needs to finger them, or play a single glissando.

Awkward Connection

As in the following passage, there are some quick position changes which are rather awkward. The best way to practice is to play the last two thirds as a four-note chord and go to the next fz chord as quickly as possible. Know the hand position on the keys where you finish the ascending, wrist out on a black note, and then come into the lower third (A and C). One must know exactly how much hand rotation is to be involved. When the change of position feels better, then add another 3rd in front and in back one by one. The minute any tension is felt, locate and loosen it. Tension is not only an obstacle, it can cause bad tone as well as physical damage in some cases.

Example 3.16. Chopin Ballade, Op. 52.

Transfer from Right to Left Hand

Most of us have a weaker left hand. When the left hand has difficulty playing a passage, reverse the passage (mirror version) for the right hand and see how it feels to play it with the right hand. Normally it is much easier for the right hand to play. Then transfer that sensation to the left hand. One can also practice hands together (in reverse position). The left hand learns the technique much quicker thus getting rid of the difficulty.

Fingering

Some awkward passages will cease to be difficult when one finds the right fingering. Always figure out where the fingers go to rather than where they come from. One should avoid jerky motion in any direction, being there before playing.

The following are some examples with octave skips. In preparation for the leap to the fifth finger, it is best to have the thumb on the previous note in preparation, especially when the interval is an octave or larger. One never misses the fifth finger bass notes this way.

Example 3.17. Chopin Etude, Op. 10 #12.

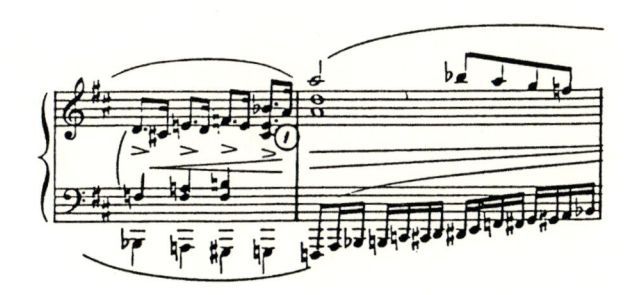

Example 3.18. Chopin, Sonata, Op. 58, 1st Movement.

When the previous note is the same as a note in the following chord, use the same finger as in the chord so that the same finger remains on the same note, avoiding a quick change of position.

Example 3.19. Chopin Prelude, Op. 28, #18.

Below is another example of fingering in preparation of what is to follow. In anticipation of double trill fingering, change the single trill fingering 2 3 to 2 1 ahead of time so that the top trill can be added with no disturbance.

Example 3.20. Chopin Barcarolle, Op. 60.

The reverse can be seen in the following example. Even though it may interrupt the finger legato in the melody, it is much safer to use the fifth finger in anticipation of the next chord. It eliminates the skip, resulting in a sharp rhythm.

Example 3.21. Debussy, Prelude, Book 1, "Les collines d'Anacapri"

For a brilliant fast passage, as in Example 3.22, rather than using the standard fingering of 1 2 3 4 1 2 3 4 5, 1 2 3 1 2 3 4 1 5 gives much stronger articulation. In other words, avoid using 3 4 5 if possible for brilliancy.

Example 3.22. Chopin, Etude, Op. 10 #4.

On the other hand, when a smooth legato is called for, one can achieve a better tone by stretching the fingers with a lateral rotation using all fingers 1 - 5 and/or substituting fingers. Crossing fingers with the thumb should be avoided at all costs because it makes the weight transfer more difficult for a real legato.

Example 3.23. Chopin Nocturne, Op. 27, #1.

For legato passages, as mentioned earlier, substitution (changing fingers while holding down a note) is highly recommended, especially in contrapuntal writing. It is a good idea always to practice the melodic lines without the pedal, since the tone will be completely different when it is played as a finger legato or connected only by the use of the pedal.

Playing with Crossed Hands

Try crossing the hands on your lap or a table top. The second finger reaches further than the thumb, so that it is best to use the second finger or the third finger when reaching across even on the black keys. Use the thumbs only when a heavy tone is desirable.

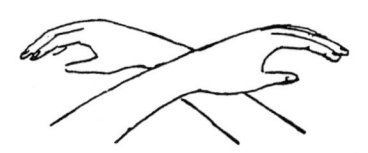

Figure 3.11. Crossed hand position.

Hand Switching

In preparation for really wide leaps, when applicable, take the previous note(s) with the other hand to give more time for the hand to get to the position. In the following example it is also possible to take the last two octaves (D and E$^{\flat}$) with the left hand.

Example 3.24 Chopin Scherzo, Op. 31.

There is an art to switching hands as in the case of the following example, Debussy's Prelude, "Feux d'Artifice." It will be practically impossible to have the triplets without a slight break before the high octave at the fast tempo if played as written, but this switching makes it sound as though it is being played with three hands.

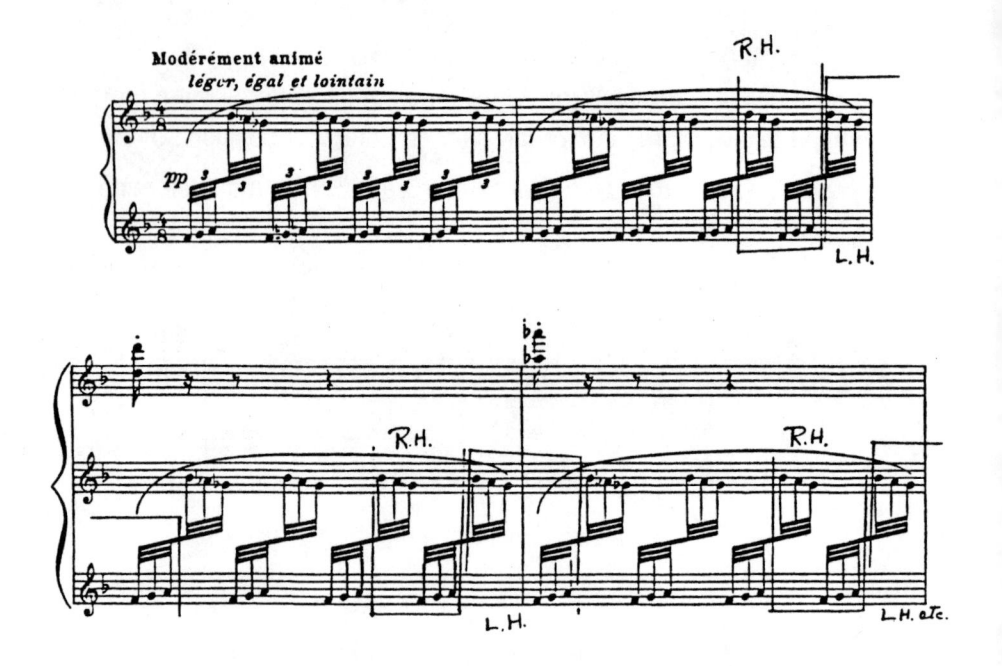

Example 3.25 Debussy Prelude Book II, "Feux d'Artifice"

"It does not matter which fingering one uses as long as it sounds beautiful." -- Cécile Genhart.

Chapter 4

MELODY AND HARMONY

Regrouping

Music flows from beat to beat as one foot follows the other in walking. As soon as the motion starts on the beat, it has to move to the next. In other words, there should never be a break before the beat except for rare occasions like a hesitation before the climactic chord for emphasis.

Regrouping refers to rephrasing the notes in between beats to make the inflection, shading and direction clearer, and at the same time, avoiding squareness. Notes between the beats are either resolution (or slur-off) and/or upbeats leading to the next beat. It is necessary to figure out what is important (or more beautiful) and what is not. The following example shows two possible ways of regrouping. Choose whichever feels natural.

Example 4.1. Schumann, "Eusebius" from Carnaval, Op. 9.

Regrouping is also used to help the flow of the music. The next example has three possibilities.

Example 4.2. Chopin Etude, Op. 25 #1.

1. is the simplest division, flowing from beat to beat;
2. is recommended if one has difficulty moving into the note after the beat;
3. makes the best sense tonally since both thumb notes create beautiful harmonic thirds.

It is advisable to practice in various ways, mastering the ones that are harder.

Rephrasing also helps some ascending or descending thirds sound smoother and more melodious.

Example 4.3. Mozart Sonata, K. 333, 2nd Movement.

Even for the ascending thirds, going to the beat in seconds sounds more beautiful.

Example 4.4. Mozart, Variations on Menuet by Duport.

It also helps to make awkward intervals in melody smoother, yet more intense.

Example 4.5. Beethoven Sonata, Op. 110, 1st Movement.

Some skips can be practiced regrouped. Be sure to overlap the groups in fast technical passages to secure good connection.

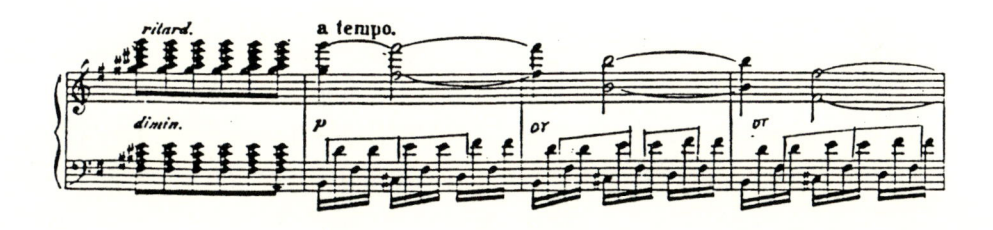

Example 4.6. Beethoven Sonata, Op. 90, 1st Movement.

And finally, it makes voicing clearer. The chromatic line starting from A to E# comes alive in the following example.

Example 4.7. Chopin Scherzo, Op. 39.

Treatment of Melody

<u>Continuation</u>

Singing a melodic line beautifully is one of the most essential qualities in music making. Singers and instrumentalists can even swell on a long note. Unfortunately for pianists, the tone diminishes after the initial stroke. In order for the melody to sustain a smooth line, keen listening is imperative to match the amount of sound left on the long note when the succeeding note is played. However, it does not mean that a diminuendo takes place because one can increase in volume right away on the following notes, though it is a good idea to give enough tone to the long notes when musically applicable to ensure that the tone will last.

Figure 4.1.

All three A^b's in the next example follow the long notes. One needs to listen carefully to the long notes on the second beat (tied notes) to hear how much sound is left, then match the following A^b for a smooth connection. After the first A^b, start the crescendo to the next downbeat, which is quite appropriate to the music in the example.

Example 4.8. Beethoven, Sonata, Op. 13, 2nd Movement.

Sing Through the Long Note

It is uncanny to hear the difference when a long note is sung through to the next note and when the mind leaves the note while the sound is held merely by a finger and/or pedaling. One cannot emphasize the importance of singing through the entire value of long notes with intensity and often with crescendo to make up for the decay in tone, otherwise the melodic line or harmonic progression becomes weak or broken. By intending crescendo on long notes when there is accompaniment figuration, the intensity can be carried over in the accompaniment to make a significant difference. Continuation always needs to take place on the following note, but with the support in the accompaniment, one can get away with the minimum amount of continuation.

Example 4.9. Beethoven, Sonata, Op. 31, #3, 3rd Movement.

Wide Leaps

When a melodic line has a big leap, the tone of the first should match with the second as in a slur-off. The use of the slur-off touch helps to make a nice connection. The second note will be surprisingly softer than the first whichever direction it goes.

Example 4.10. Beethoven, Sonata, Op. 2, #2, 4th Movement.

Approach to the high notes. When asked, students often point to the highest note of the melodic line as the climax of the phrase. They often play the high note the loudest with little consideration of where strong beats fall or the importance of the harmonic progression. By nature, the high notes are apt to stand out. To avoid the accentuation, one needs to play the note before the highest equally loud and sing up (slur up) to the high note. When the interval is wide, take time in doing so as singers do.

Example 4.11. Bach, Invention in C Minor.

If a crescendo is involved, crescendo to the note preceding the highest note and keep the volume the same on the high note. If emphasis is called for as the high point of the phrase, instead of playing it louder, cling to it a little longer as in lyrical singing.

Inflection and Shading

As in speaking, one emphasizes a particular point, changing the tone of one's voice in a sentence according to the importance or the expression of the words. The same goes in singing a melodic line. If it is a four-measure phrase, there are normally two or three color changes. One should keep in mind where the climax of the phrase falls, then break the phrase down to shorter segments.

Example 4.12. Chopin, Nocturne, Op. 27, #2.

In the peaceful, gentle atmosphere, the first segment starts with much sincerity, perhaps with a touch of melancholy. Segment two is more relaxed and warm, leading into an intense, grander declamation (climax) on B^b in the third segment. As in most sequences, the ending of the third segment is repeated in the fourth, but is more gentle (or weary) in this case. The final segment, the fifth, has a rich A natural resolving quietly on B^b.

The above description is only one interpretation. Each pianist must decide what he/she wants to do. The inflection and coloring become very obvious when one knows exactly how each segment is to be expressed.

Question and Answer

Some melodies sound as Question and Answer within one phrase. They can often be treated as a duet between male and female voices, or big and small ensemble groups, changing in color and expression. Do not hesitate to make them obviously different, though they should be played as one phrase.

Example 4.13. Mozart Sonata K. 576, 1st Movement.

Example 4.14. Haydn Sonata, Hob. XVI, 23, 1st Movement.

Tied Notes

Make sure the tied note is held to the following one without a break in sound. Tied notes on the beat, if played on instruments such as the violin or oboe, can be sung with emphasis, which the music often calls for. Pianists should try to create the same effect by intending a crescendo, singing through the note to the tied note and slurring off on the succeeding note. Often the tied notes are somewhat held over, but unfortunately not sung or held to the following note.

Example 4.15. Chopin, Nocturne, Op. 48, #1.

Melody Consisting of Repeated Notes or Notes of the Same Note Value

Repeated notes in a melody need more inflection and freedom in time (rubato) to give them a sense of direction and form, otherwise they are apt to sound monotonous. Regrouping of the notes gives them the shape and flow of direction.

Example 4.16. Liszt, Sonata in B Minor.

When melody notes are mostly quarter notes or eighth notes, for example, they also require more emphasis in inflection, direction and rubato, as in repeated notes to make them more interesting.

Trill Figuration

The same goes for the trill or similar figuration in melody, as in the following example.

Example 4.17. Chopin Ballade, Op. 52.

Since the melody hovers within the short intervals of thirds or fourths, it needs more inflection especially on the trill figuration in the sixteenth notes. Regrouping often works but it is imperative to avoid grouping in 2 and 2 which makes them sound square. Always divide 1 and 3 or 3 and 1, as in the above example.

Ornaments

When playing any melodic line with ornaments, it is helpful to first remove them all and learn the basic line with the most suitable expression (inflection, dynamics, color changes, and subtle rubato, etc.). Then insert the ornament to enhance the expression. One plays many more notes as ornaments in place of one note, often on weak beats or even between beats. In order not to disturb the melodic line, ornaments need to be played very lightly to fit in smoothly.

Turns

In the music of the Baroque and early Classical periods, and even in some of the Romantic period, the turns generally start with the upper notes on the beat. However, in melodious passages as those in the Romantic period, it is more graceful to start the turn right after the accompaniment note. In other words, do not play the first note of the turn together or the beat.

Example 4.18. Chopin Nocturne, Op. 27, #2.

Grace Notes

Grace notes also are there to make the melodic line more delicate and graceful, as the name suggests. They are to be played lightly and quickly so as not to disturb the melody. However, occasionally the important melodic line is written out by composers as grace notes when the reach is too wide for the hand to hold down the notes.

Example 4.19. Beethoven, Sonata, Op. 2, #2, 1st Movement.

In the above example, the alto canon is indicated as grace notes, which should be played with good tone as in the other voices. Another example can be seen as an important bass line in the following example.

Example 4.20. Beethoven Sonata, Op. 101, 3rd Movement.

Syncopation

Always come late on syncopation. It is there for emphasis in expression, often for the effect of deep pathos or anticipation. In any case, it has a very strong emotional impact. Rather than playing it louder, because the accent is almost always ugly, play the syncopated notes slightly late. The hesitation not only makes the tone more focused but also helps the rest of the phrase to flow better.

Example 4.21. Chopin, Nocturne, Op. 48, #1.

Triplets

When triplets are written as a part of the slow melodic line, they are seldom played evenly. Instead, a rubato is applied, though it should be done very subtly so that it sounds natural.

Example 4.22. Chopin, Waltz, Op. 69. #1.

When two or more sets of triplets occur, they tend to sound grouped as 3 plus 3. To avoid the awkwardness, regroup them together as a six note figuration, applying one rubato to blend them as a flowing phrase.

Example 4.23. Schumann, "In der Nacht" from Fantasiestucke, Op. 12.

The same goes with combination of odd-numbered groups. Rubato and regrouping are very useful to minimize metric regularity.

Example 4.24. Mozart, "Variations on a Minuet by Duport"

We have two sets of triplets in the second and third measures. A little rubato (and continuation) after the tied notes on the second beat not only smooths the melodic line but makes the musical flow easier and freer, pushing towards the highest notes which, in this case, should be approached delicately. After the highest notes, take time (another touch of rubato) on three upbeats leading back to the more important long notes on the downbeats. Listeners should not be aware that these notes were written as 3 + 3 + 4 (2 + 2), though rubato needs to be very subtle.

Cadenza Figuration (Added Notes in Fast Passages)

When there are many more notes in the melodic line than in the accompaniment figuration, never try to divide the notes mathematically, as mentioned earlier. This does not work since we sing taking more time on the first few notes of the group, moving through the middle of a group lightly generally faster and taking time on the last few notes to sing out to the final note or next melody.

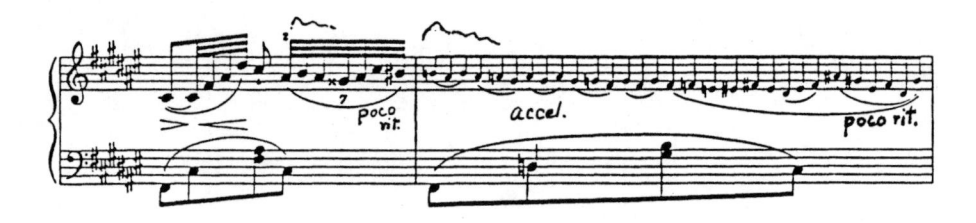

Example 4.25. Chopin, Nocturne, Op. 15, #2.

Slurs

Generally, short slurs (2 or 3 notes) are to be played long, short or long, long - short. Since the ending short note is heard only for an instant, even though the notes are played alike, the long note tends to sound louder than the short note. For this reason, it is important to give enough clarity to the short note especially in fast tempo. There are endless varieties of expression in slurs, starting with agitated excitement, restlessness, sadness, etc.

For restless anxiety, there is the opening of the Tempest Sonata. Use of the fingering 3 2, 3 2 will make the notes sound evenly and there is no need to think of playing long, short, long, short. The fingering will do it.

Example 4.26. Beethoven, Sonata, Op. 31, #2, 1st Movement.

Also restless, but in the background as sobbing is seen in the following example. In this case, short notes should be played somewhat softer.

Example 4.27. Beethoven, Sonata, Op. 13, 2nd Movement.

One of the most expressive melodies, choked with sadness, will be heard in the following aria. Since the tempo is slow enough, the short note should be played softer, without losing clarity.

Example 4.28. Beethoven, Sonata, Op. 110, 3rd Movement.

Bebung. Also from the same movement, Beethoven uses *bebung*, a clavichord technique. This is a rare exception when the long note is to be played louder and the short note extremely soft.

Example 4.29. Beethoven, Sonata, Op. 110, 3rd Movement.

And in accompaniment,

Example 4.30. Chopin, Prelude, Op. 28, #6.

Since Chopin indicates the first long note to be emphasized with an accent, the second short note should be played quite softly as in a sigh.

Slurs can also express exuberant happiness as in this example.

Example 4.31. Beethoven, Sonata, Op. 81a, 3rd Movement.

What a different expression would result without the slurs!

Inverted Slur

Inverted slurs (slurs which end on beats) are quite insistent. They go against the beat, therefore it is natural that they sound determined, agitated or defiant, etc. They should be played with crescendo to the beat (short notes).

Example 4.32. Beethoven, Sonata, Op. 14, #2, 1st Movement.

Voicing and Coloring

In unison passages, it is seldom that one plays both lines alike except in f passages. For a dark, rich, mysterious, etc. effect, it is often suitable to favor the lower line. For a bright, sad, or gentle quality, one favors the top line. It gives a much wider range of expression when divided as in the following example.

Example 4.33. Schumann, "Papillons," Op. 2.

In some melodic lines, it is important to separate voices. In the following example, the sonorous harmonies with the melody on top (B^b, B^b, A, etc.) should be sung through the rests in mind, though the pedal needs to be cleared. The soprano comes in with completely different color and expression. If one sings down, up, down, up as one melody line, the solemn intensity of the long main melody will be lost.

Example 4.34. Beethoven, Sonata, Op. 31, #2, 2nd Movement.

The same idea can be seen in the following example. The first Forte chord continues to the third measure over the rests, resulting in p as written out continuation.

Example 4.35. Beethoven, Sonata, Op. 10, #1, 1st Movement.

There are occasions when a melody shifts registers, as in the following melody in thirds. Needless to say that the long notes must slur up or down to the following notes in order to make the awkward skips smooth and melodious.

Example 4.36. Beethoven, Sonata, Op. 10, #1, 1st Movement.

Also in the same example, the descending bass melody has harmonic notes inserted which should be played softer as slur-offs, keeping the (bass) melody line continuous.

In some fast passages one needs to find a basic line among all the notes in order to avoid a mass of sound, as follows.

Example 4.37. Chopin, Ballade, Op. 52.

In any melodic line, one should be aware of the basic melody notes--"the skeleton"--so that the main inflection is always based on that line with less importance on extraneous notes. In the following example, the circled notes are the skeleton and dotted circled notes indicate secondary important notes. The melody ends at * in the second measure. The following chromatic alto line is nothing but the link which should be played much lighter leading into the repeat of the main theme. The tone quality, the volume and inflection should be determined according to the importance of each note, thus making the whole melodic line cohesive.

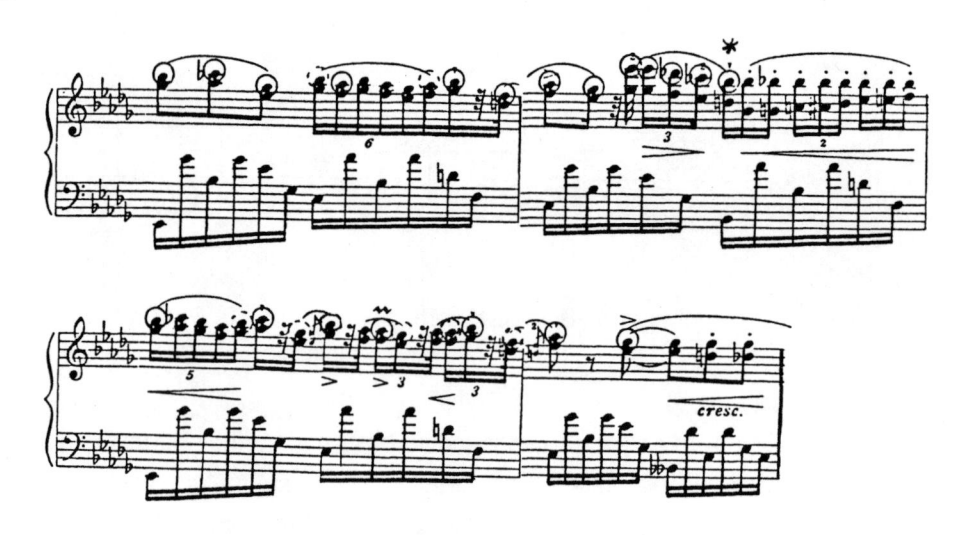

Example 4.38. Chopin, Nocturne, Op. 27, #2.

How often does one hear the following from Schumann's Papillons played as though ascending and descending arpeggios are two completely different passages. It should all sound as a melodic line in one big sweep. It is beneficial to practice a passage of this sort (descending here) with both thumbs, connecting as legato and melodicas possible, then add light fifth fingers.

Example 4.39. Schumann, Papillons, Op. 2.

Occasionally music does not indicate the melodic line. One needs to rely on the ear rather than the eyes, especially in French music as in the following illustrations.

Example 4.40. Ravel, Toccata from "Tombeau de Couperin"

Example 4.41. Ravel, Alborada del Gracioso from "Miroirs"

Harmony

Harmony is often neglected, especially in contrapuntal writing. Even though the melodic lines are individually beautifully sung, voices should also harmonize with each other in color, inflection and balance, as in fine ensemble playing. It will be most beneficial to practice slowly, listening to the direction, inflection and the nuances of the harmonic progression. Especially in the fast passages the harmonic accompaniment has a tendency to become merely rhythmic emphasis. Always match and make the harmonies come alive as in the following example.

Example 4.42. Chopin, Etude, Op. 10, #4.

Very often the notes on the beat are either appogiatura, suspension, or passing notes. They are placed to give more color and emphasis. As in any dissonance, they can sound harsh or ugly if played too loudly but they also can be beautiful resolving to the harmonic notes. Listen to them blend with the rest of the harmonies. Cécile Genhart used to say, "Play to the Harmony."

Example 4.43. Chopin, Fantasia, Op. 49.

Example 4.44. Mozart, Sonata, K. 576, 1st Movement.

Crossing Thumbs

The Romantic composers, especially Chopin and Schumann, often wrote thumbs crossed, making the playing a little more difficult in big chords or arpeggios. Yet the sounds one gets from crossed thumbs are much richer since they are supported by the weight of the whole hand. If, for ease, one switches the fingers, make sure that both thumbs get the same rich weighty tone.

Example 4.45. Schumann, Sonata, Op. 22, 1st Movement.

Example 4.46. Chopin, Etude, Op. 25, #1.

Alberti Bass

First, play through blocking the chords (play all notes simultaneously) to feel the hand position and more importantly to learn and hear the harmonic progression. The bass line is also very important. It should be brought out as an independent melodic line with the right inflection and appropriate tone, but often there are hidden inner melodic line(s). These moving voices are often beautiful, especially when they harmonize with the main melody. This can be best worked out by playing the inner melodies or bass melody, whichever one plans to favor, with one hand and the other less important notes with the other hand to hear the inflection and the proper balance, then learn to reproduce the same with one hand. When one starts to play accompaniments without going through this learning process, neither the balance, nuance, nor the inflection is ever good enough.

Example 4.47. Beethoven, Op. 14, #2, 1st Movement.

Rolled Chords

There is no rule as to when to start rolling and when to finish, except to find the beauty of the sound. However, the following suggestions can be made, according to the nature of the sound, since notes harmonize better within narrower intervals. They start to separate when the intervals become widen than tenth. Inner notes serve as 'glue' to hold the outer notes together as a harmony.

When the Rolled Chord is in the Left Hand: (1) Make sure that the bass note is held in the pedal, otherwise one can end up in inversions much against the composer's intent, and (2) If time permits, the last (highest) note goes together with the right-hand notes. Therefore the left hand needs to start rolling before the beat. The pedal also needs to be taken on the bass note before the beat. In order not to blur the melody notes, it would be ideal to hold the bass notes with the fingers as long as possible and catch the sound with the pedal at the last instant.

Example 4.48. Schumann, Carnaval, Op. 9, Eusebius.

When the Rolled Chord is in the Right Hand: It starts together with the left-hand note on the beat since the first note of the rolled chord blends together with the left-hand note much more beautifully than the last note (highest note) of the chord.

Example 4.49. Brahms, Intermezzo, Op. 118, #2.

When the Roll is Continuous: It should be rolled from the bottom up from the bass note (Left Hand) to the highest note (Right Hand).

Broken Roll: If the roll is broken between hands, both hands are to be rolled together. However, rather than starting and ending the hands together, the sound is more beautiful when the left hand starts slightly ahead and the right hand top note finishes last, thus preventing the inner notes from sounding together.

There are many exceptions to the above suggestions. The broken rolls are often rolled as a continuous roll as in the example below. Since each case is different, one needs to experiment with various ways to find the most beautiful.

Example 4.50. Debussy, Suite Bergamasque, "Clair de Lune."

Chapter 5

SALIENT INTERPRETATIONAL EXPRESSIONS

Some Musical Concepts

Playing Crescendo and Diminuendo

The mountain is steeper if one climbs from the foot rather than starting in the middle. In other words, start a crescendo as softly as appropriate and do not start the diminuendo until after the indication. "Think p when you see crescendo. Think f when you see diminuendo." Also, when dramatic quality is called for, delay the application so that the build-up will be more effective. The same applies to a diminuendo, only in reverse. Often the climax does not come through effectively because the moment it is reached the diminuendo starts. Instead, stay big as long as possible and enjoy the melodic shading and harmonic nuances in the diminuendo towards the end. Change of tonal qualities become more difficult in the p level.

Figure 5.1. Playing crescendo and diminuendo.

Long Crescendo

When a very long crescendo is called for, it is best to start the crescendo in the melodic line first, followed later by the accompaniment. For diminuendo the accompaniment should start first and be followed by the melody to be out of the way.

Example 5.1. Chopin, Etude, Op. 25, #11.

Example 5.2. Beethoven, Sonata, Op. 81a, 3rd Movement.

Hemiola

Why do they exist? Mozart, Beethoven, Chopin and Brahms in particular used hemiola a great deal to create rhythmical excitement. Since the regular rhythm needs to be facilitated, as in the following example, 3 + 3 in 3/4 time changes to 2 + 2 + 2. The best way to treat it is to switch the bar lines.

Example 5.3. Mozart, Sonata, K. 332, 1st Movement.

In the following example, rather than playing in 3/4 time, think as 2/4 in hemiola. It is a great relief to go back to 3/4 time after the breathless, unsettled feeling created by hemiola.

Example 5.4. Chopin, Scherzo, Opus 39

Rests

Rests play a very important role both rhythmically and melodically, yet one has a tendency to count the rests too fast, faster than the regular notes. They should be felt with an accent, especially when they fall on the beats, to ensure the duration. In general, the note(s) preceding the rest should be released exactly on the rest to make it rhythmically clear. Beethoven uses rests in a unique way at the end of his pieces. Often he writes an extra measure with a rest and sometimes even with a fermata over it. In these cases, there should be no retard on the last chords since that will spoil the intended momentum of the rhythmic vitality and the sense of "going on."

Example 5.5. Beethoven, Sonata, Op. 2, #2, 1st Movement

Dotted Rhythm

"Long note long, short note short."

For a lively effect, hold the dotted note a little longer than its duration, making the following short note shorter. Only a subtle touch of this makes a big difference in the rhythm.

Dotted Rhythm in Slow Melodic Line.

"Long note long enough and short note also long enough" applies to a dotted rhythm in melodic passages. Make sure to sing the short note with care. They are often casually skipped over.

Chopin is quite meticulous in indicating dotted rhythms in two ways. When written as a dotted eighth and sixteenth, they should be played legato in time, but an eighth followed by a sixteenth rest and a sixteenth note should be played with more exaggeration, bouncing up on the rest, delaying the last sixteenth to make the rhythm lighter and sharper.

Example 5.6. Chopin, Fantaisie, Op. 49.

Orchestral Conception

There are numerous passages in the piano music which sound very much like the orchestra, especially in Mozart, Haydn, Beethoven, Schubert, Liszt and Brahms. For instance most of Beethoven's sonatas and variations need to be orchestrated in our minds. In thinking orchestrally, the coloring will become clearer and the dynamics more three-dimensional as solo melody versus tutti. In choosing a particular solo instrument, not only the color becomes more definite but the expression and inflection are more evident, whereas the tutti demands sonority as well as rhythmic precision.

Particular Use of Forte and Piano

Often in the early Classical period as in Haydn and Mozart, there are generally only two dynamic markings--f and p. Forte does not always mean loud nor piano soft. They are to be treated as expressions. Forte can be lively or stately, for example (but never too thick). Piano can be sad, gentle, warm, etc., differing in color and feeling.

Example 5.7. Mozart, Sonata, K. 570, 1st Movement.

In the above example, if the second f passage (C Major) were played suddenly loudly, it would be quite unmusical, especially as the downbeat is the conclusion of the previous phrase. Furthermore, the main melody of the new section does not start until the third beat, which is only the upbeat. The character changes from lyrical to lively, hence the brighter sound is called for but a big tone is not appropriate, especially in the accompaniment.

Subito Piano

Subito p takes a little hesitation before in order for the forte sound to diminish completely. If played on time, the p tone will be smeared. Also, make sure to keep the clarity in the melody while the harmony changes to become suddenly soft. In other words, subito p takes place in the accompaniment but not much in the melody. When the melody is also played softly, the clarity and the intensity can be lost as well.

Accent

"Think of accent as emphasis in expression" (Frank Mannheimer). Accent is often indicated to clarify the melodic line or in place of tenuto. One needs only to bring the line out, but not punch the notes out. When placed singly, take good care of the note. In melodic passages, cling to it longer or replace it with a slight hesitation, whichever is more suitable. Often the use of the staccato pedal serves the purpose nicely without playing louder.

Sforzando

Sf is a musical emphasis, the same as in accent, except always stay within the dynamic levels. Sf in p should be played as mp, sf in mf as f. Sf can be treated with a touch of pedal for tonal emphasis.

Favor the Third

A third of a chord is the essence of the harmony. In any triad, if the third is favoured, the whole harmony comes alive. Without the third, there are only the fourth, fifth and octave, all of which are not harmonious. If there is a seventh, that is beautiful also. Always know where the third (and seventh) is and take special care.

Inner Notes

"Inner notes are glue to hold harmonies together" (Frank Mannheimer). When playing a chord or a broken harmony with both hands, make sure both thumbs harmonize and match with the rest of the harmony. When inner voices are neglected, the chords separate, failing to harmonize.

More Tone in Slow Pieces

More sound is needed in slow pieces, otherwise the tone as well as the intensity will be lost. This is especially true in some Adagio or Grave movements by Beethoven where the pulsation is very slow. Even though p may be indicated use as much weight as appropriate to help sustain the tone, and sing through with much intensity.

Timing

For orchestra members, it is very critical that they play precisely together. No one dares to come too early or too late. Pianists need to do the same in <u>timing</u> every note. This precision calls for focusing one's mind, emotion, physical action and keen listening to one instance, requiring the utmost concentration. This results in clear and intense projection.

Stage Whisper

Actors whisper with good intensity if each word is to be heard. The same goes for the piano. Never play too softly but keep the intensity in each note, especially in the melody. This is particularly true when playing in a big hall as neither the tone nor the message will carry to the audience if the tone becomes spongy. "Play to the last row in Carnegie Hall" was said many times by Mrs. Genhart. Projection is often neglected in teaching by non-performing teachers.

Virtue of Slow Practicing

When first learning a piece, it is important to never make a single mistake. This keeps bad habits from developing in one's mind, ear, and technique. This can be done only by very slow practicing. When playing, focus the mind, heart (expression or feeling), and physical action into one precise moment. In this way, one's entire being is focused into the sound. Always use keen listening but be physically relaxed and ready. In the course of slow practicing, emphasize each nuance, inflection, balance, clarity, etc. in a very exaggerated manner--like looking through a magnifying glass.

Dynamic levels should be exaggerated and color changes in their extremes. Without the exaggeration, there will not be enough nuances, colors, dynamics, etc. when one picks up the tempo. The depth will not be deep enough, the tone may not be rich enough. One should aim for 200% in slow practice so that every note will come alive at the proper tempo. However, it is very important that one plays the passage at a fast tempo occasionally to feel the correct physical sensation. If only slow practice is done, the touch used there may be quite different from what it actually should be. After a while, combine slow and faster (and lighter) practice, to facilitate the progress. Endurance also needs to be built up gradually to a tempo or even to faster tempo.

Finally, it is very critical to develop one's own way of practicing. This helps to develop one's originality and creativity. Also, one must cultivate his/her unique tone quality. Some people naturally have rich sound, some have clear sound, others gentle or even a dull sound. It is important to know one's own tone quality so that one can develop those which are not inherent in one's makeup. One must not fall into the habit of using this natural sound all of the time but one must choose the tone which is most appropriate to the particular note being played.

Definition of Some Musical Terms

Rubato

The word "rubato" is of German origin and akin to the Old High German "roubon," to rob, which comes from the Latin "rubare" meaning to steal. It is applied to steal time. There are two kinds of rubato: (1) leaning on rubato, and (2) pushing on rubato.

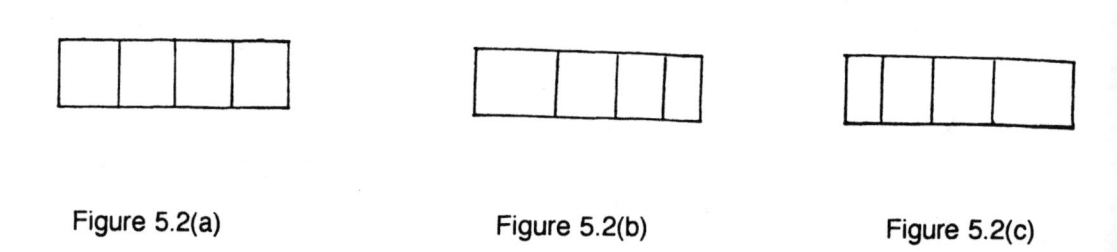

Figure 5.2(a)   Figure 5.2(b)   Figure 5.2(c)

Equal duration on each quarter note in 4/4 time is indicated in (a) while (b) illustrates leaning on rubato, taking more time at the beginning of the measure and making it up at the end so that the next downbeat will come together as in (a). Pushing on rubato is illustrated in (c). This is just the reverse of leaning on rubato. In either case, the rubato can be done on a beat (subdivided by sixteenth), or even over several measures. The characteristic is to gradually make up whatever has been done in time, unlike accelerando or ritardando. Rubato is employed constantly in lyrical passages.

Tremolo

Measured and free. Generally speaking, if the lines are connected to the stems it should be played measured as thirtyseconds (since there are three lines indicating thirtyseconds) as in the following example.

Example 5.8. Ravel, Jeux d'eau.

When the lines are detached, it is a free tremolo.

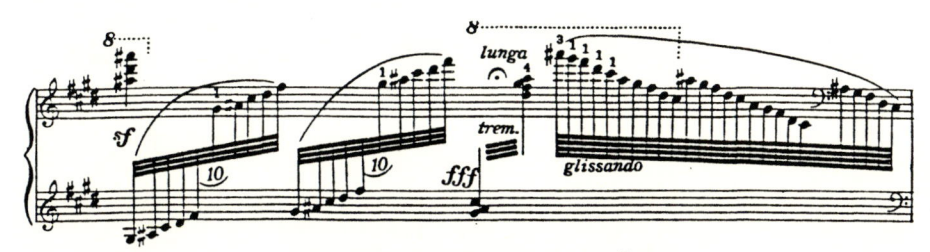

Example 5.9. Ravel, Jeux d'eau.

There are quite a few exceptions to the rules.
Con Anima
This is often treated the same as <u>animato</u>. However, con anima means "with soul." Chopin was especially fond of con anima with exceptionally beautiful melodies. We would express it as singing your heart out.
Sostenuto
Sostenuto means to sustain the sound. In Brahms this means not only to hold the tone but to slow the tempo.
Ritardando, Rallentando, and Ritenuto
These are quite loosely used by many composers, but strictly used by some, as Beethoven, Chopin and particularly Debussy. Whereas ritardando and rallentando mean to gradually slow down, ritenuto means to play in the slower tempo as in un poco meno mosso. Also it is a general feeling that ritardando does mean more slowing down than rallentando. Debussy was most particular in indicating each, ending up with *cedez*, which means a slight slowing down.

In order to make a ritardando or rallentando evenly, one should feel the smallest pulsation or subdivision of the beat. This makes the gradation much more beautifully controlled. Make sure that the ritard is felt over the rests as well.

Example 5.10. Schumann, "Träumerei" from "Scenes from Childhood," Op. 15

Breath Marking

Two short diagonal lines by Debussy is often mistaken as a breath sign. It only indicates the end of the previous sign as ritardando, cedez, or serrez and no pause should be placed here. Debussy uses a comma to indicate a breath, as do some other contemporary composers.

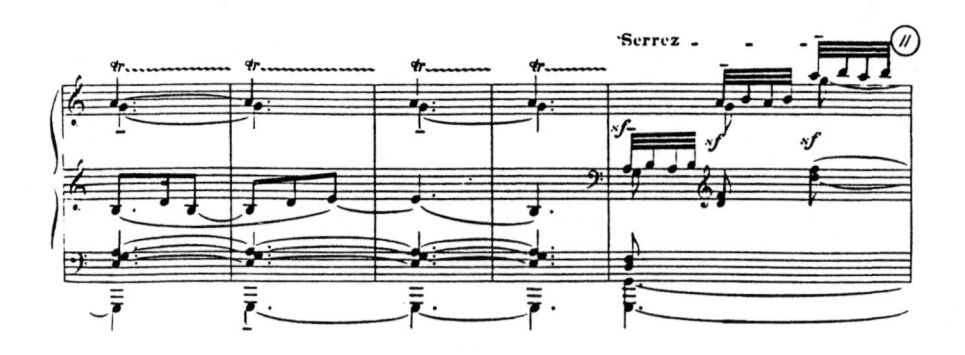

Example 5.11. Debussy, Prelude "Les faes sont e'exquises danseuses"

Chapter 6

EXERCISES

This chapter gives some exercises for stretching the hand, correcting a double-jointed thumb, strengthening the first joint of the fingers, and releasing weight and tension.

Stretching Exercises

Stretching must be done daily, ideally several times a day, for a short period of time or one loses the gains made. Never do stretching exercises with cold hands as injury may result. Any exercise should be done with extreme care and concentration. When feeling tiredness in any muscle if it feels warm/comfortable, one can safely keep going with caution. If any sharp pain is felt, stop immediately. This is a sign that a tendon is being strained. Some experts suggest that ice be put on the tendon immediately but it is safest to consult a reliable physician to determine the appropriate treatment. Tendonitis can recur easily unless it is taken care of completely at its inception.

1. The safest and easiest exercise is to stretch one hand as much as possible, spreading the fingers in all directions, hold them there and count to ten slowly. Then make a fist (the reverse of stretching) and count to ten again. Repeat these two exercises ten times in succession. Do this several times throughout the day. Stretching should always be done to both sides of the hands.

2. Another easy and safe exercise is to rub lightly but quickly the webs of the fingers including the long web between the thumb and index finger. Rub the web with one, two or three fingers--as many as there is room for--until the skin turns pink. Be very careful to keep the hand relaxed.

Figure 6.1. Stretching exercise.

If the skin is dry use some hand lotion to soften the skin. It makes it easier and more comfortable. Since this exercise loosens the whole hand, this is a very good warming-up exercise as well.

   3. Take any 5-note chord, perhaps starting with a diminished seventh chord, minor-minor seventh, major-minor seventh or their inversions. Play each note, bottom up, as a forte melody tone, getting hold of each note <u>without using weight</u>.

      a. Hold all notes without sticking, and trill two fingers in any order. Work on the difficult combinations.

      b. Also holding down, play given two notes in dotted rhythm.

      c. With the left hand, play 5 and 3 together, 4 and 2 together, 3 and 1 together back and forth. Reverse for the right hand. Be sure to use the finger tips, producing good tone.

      d. Do the above exercise in dotted rhythm. When the chords mentioned above become easy, take major-major seventh or even augmented chords to stretch. Do them in all keys. Each hand to be played carefully with a loose wrist.

   4. The following is Cécile Genhart's warming-up exercise with good stretch. Get hold of each note in a slow, marcato touch, the wrist to be rotated to support each finger being played.

Example 6.1. Arpeggio exercise

   5. The following is Frank Mannheimer's exercise. This is extremely stretchy. When done correctly, one can stretch to reach another key in just a few weeks' time, though it must be done with the utmost caution.

Hold silently

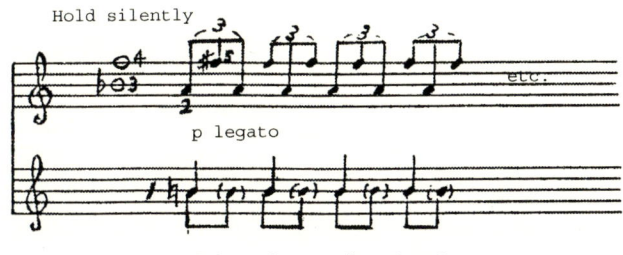

p legato

Play on beat, then 2 x 3

Example 6.2. Frank Mannheimer's exercise.

For the right hand:
- a. Hold B^b and F (if too stretchy, try E or even E^b to start with) silently with 3 and 4 with the fingers completely stretched (flat tips). If it is difficult to hold them down, use the other hand (fingers) to hold them in place.
- b. Play A with 2 and F# with 5 as triplets in legato lightly.
- c. Place the thumb on B under 2 and 3. Play on each beat as a quarter note indicated in the lower staff.
- d. Play the thumb as duplets (eighth notes), making the rhythm 2 x 3.
- e. Relax after a minute or two of this exercise.

One can come back to repeat the exercise every hour or two, but never continue this too long at a sitting. Never force but start as lightly as possible.

For the left hand:

The pattern should be symmetrically reversed and follow the same exercises.

(Hold B (4) and F# (3). Play triplets on G (2) A# (5) and thumb on F.)

It is beneficial to start children stretching as early as possible. Here are some useful suggestions to develop good bone structure using arpeggios, chords and octaves.
- a. Play octaves (from the side for small hands) up and down on all white keys. (If octaves are too wide, try the 7th.)
- b. Play octaves up and down on black keys.
- c. Play major and minor chords in octave position for four octaves up and down with correct fingering (r.h. 1 2 3 5, l.h. 5 4 2 1) in every key.

d. Play major and minor chords with octave chromatically up and down.
e. Play the same in inversions (r.h. 1 2 3 5, 1 2 4 5, 1 2 4 5, l.h. 5 4 2 1, 5 4 2 1, 5 3 2 1) up and down in every key.
f. Play diminished seventh chords in inversions and chromatically up and down.
g. Play the major-minor seventh chord in inversions and chromatically up and down.

Let the child work on the above exercises even though he/she may have to skip some notes. It is critical that the hands are loose. Do them lightly with caution.

Correcting the Double-Jointed Thumb

When the second joint of the thumb fails to develop, it not only hinders the independence and strength of the thumb itself, but it also restricts the reach, making it impossible to play rich chords or fast octave passages. The following are some exercises to bring out the second joint.

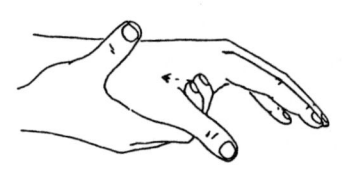

Figure 6.2. Correcting the second joint by pulling towards the wrist.

1. Relax and stretch the whole arm straight out. With the other hand, using the second and third fingers pull <u>towards the wrist</u> from <u>below</u> the second joint, which should pop the joint out. Do not pull from the second joint itself. Hold the position for a minute or two, then relax. Do this several times a day.

2. Draw a circle <u>very slowly</u> but <u>as evenly as possible</u> using only the second joint of the thumb. As shown in Figure 6.3a, first push the second joint into the hand and pull it out

gradually, (Figure 6.3b) drawing a big circle with the second joint as far out as possible. Then draw it back into the hand again. Reverse the directions.

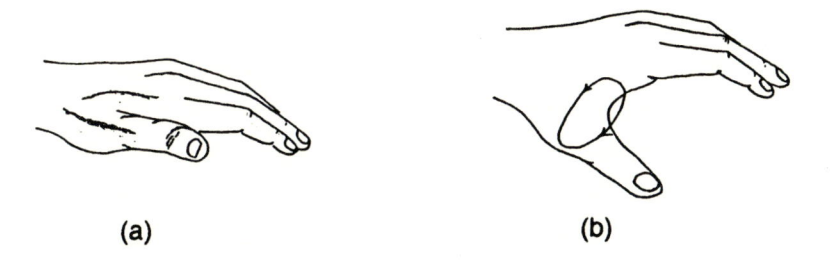

(a)   (b)

Figure 6.3. Exercises for the thumb.

Until one develops enough control over these muscles, it may be necessary to use the other hand to guide this joint. Do so in both directions. Do not tighten or move any other finger or joint while doing this exercise.

   3. At the piano, play a 5th or 6th with a thumb and a fifth finger. Place the second finger of the other hand lightly at the base of the thumb just below the second joint on the inside of the hand to bring out the second joint. Play lightly with the support of the other finger until it becomes comfortable and natural. An alternate method is to use 2 or 3 rubber bands wrapped around the thumb below the second joint. Use the other hand to pull lightly on the rubber bands towards the wrist, not out, in order to bring out the joint. Gradually increase the interval you are playing to the 7th, or octave. Play as lightly as possible in the beginning. Then decrease the support gradually until the joint stays out by itself.

Figure 6.4. Rubber band exercise.

Strengthening the First Joints

The first joint controls the speed of the key descent. It plucks, molds, bounces, etc. Some pianists emphasize the bridge of the hand. Though it is true that the bridge should be high at all times, it is the first joints which transform the speed into the sound at any dynamic level. However fast the speed created by the whole finger, if the first joints give in in contact with the tone spot, the speed will be drastically decreased, resulting in a tone which is neither bright nor clear. Therefore, it is the first joints that play the most critical role in tone quality.

1. Put both hands together (as in prayer) with the fingers pointing up. Slide one hand down exactly to the first joints of the other for support. Bend the first joint of each finger extremely slowly and smoothly as far as it will bend, being very careful not to move any other joints (Figure 6.5). Other fingers should remain completely relaxed and still. At first, it may be necessary to support the second joint with the other hand to keep it still (Figure 6.6). Gradually decrease the support until each first joint can be bent completely independently and easily.

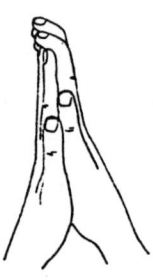

Figure 6.5. Positioning the hands.   Figure 6.6. Supporting the second joint.

2. Inchworm Exercise. Place hand, wrist and arm loose and flat on the table. Bend the first joints of the second to the fifth fingers upwards, pulling the whole hand forward (the hand and wrist are always in contact with the table). Then collapse flat like an inchworm moving forward. Repeat the exercise. At the beginning, it may be necessary to work on each finger at a time carefully. One may also need the other hand to push down at the second joints to keep them straight.

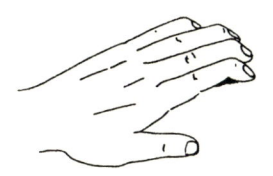

Figure 6.7. The inchworm hand position.

Exercises for Instant Key Release

So much of a heavy and dull tone is the result of sticking to the keybed (key bedding) or dropping the whole finger or whole hand as one unit rather than using the first joint to control the tone.

As explained earlier in Chapter 1 on Tone Production, the speed of the key descent at the tone spot determines the tone quality as well as the quantity. However, young students are often forced to produce bigger sounds than their little fingers are capable of, which results in pushing the key down with the whole hand. Even at a very tender age, one should be able to hear the difference in tone quality between one which rings freely and one which is forced and dull.

When using a hammer, one holds the hammer lightly in preparation to strike a nail and then gives some speed to drop the hammer head. Just before the hammer hits the nail, the hand relaxes completely. The same is true in producing a tone, otherwise the speed at the tone spot will not be the greatest. The key itself also will not be free to bounce after the tone is made. In order to get rid of the weight sticking to the key, the following exercise is effective even for very young pianists. This also makes them listen to the tone quality of each note.

Since intense concentration is required, never do both hands together. Do this very slowly with great care.

1. Relax all joints including the shoulder. Place nicely curved fingertips on the keyboard in the 5-finger position. When exercising 2 3 4 5, hold 1 lightly at the tone spot. For 4 3 2 1, hold 5.

2. In exercising the second (index) finger, hold the thumb down as lightly as possible and raise the rest of the fingers (3, 4 and 5) slightly away from the keyboard with a little curvature (Figure 6.8). Never raise them too high or have the fingers too straight to cause any tension.

Figure 6.8. Second finger exercise

3. With a firm first joint, swing the finger towards the key and bounce at the tone spot to create a light but clear ringing tone. The finger will rebound by itself if it is released as soon as the tone is made. The most important point here is that one learns to firm the first joint alone. The motion is made from the bridge, but the bridge and the 2nd joint remain loose and the hand should remain still and entirely relaxed.

4. After learning this touch, still with the same finger, play 3 staccatos slowly which should be completely alike in quality and volume, then play the fourth note with exactly the same touch, producing the same tone, but this time hold the key at the tone spot to sustain the tone. Never hold the key at the bottom. The weight of the finger should hold the key down just enough to sustain the tone. There should be no tension whatsoever. Learn to do this using the other fingers, making sure that the thumb and the little finger behave the same way -- not sideways.

5. After the above exercise becomes easy to do with every finger, do the same without the 3-staccato preparation, producing and listening to even, clear tone in legato touch.

According to Cécile Genhart who used to study composition with Ferruccio Busoni, after discovering this tone production, he retired from concertizing for a whole year in order to master this touch and its application to music, which not only enhances the tone quality significantly but also makes playing unbelievably easier.

Chapter 7

RUDIMENTS OF LEARNING AND PERFORMING

How to Learn a New Piece

Approaching a new piece is like looking at a blueprint. One must have the whole perspective before delving into the details. If the piece is unfamiliar, it is a good idea to read through it carefully or listen to a good recording once or twice to get a feel for the entire piece. (However, do not listen more than twice because one may imitate that particular interpretation without realizing it.) It is extremely important to play the work with great accuracy at the beginning because wrong notes played during this initial stage often return unexpectedly later on.

One should cherish the initial reading session. It is at this time when one's impressions are the freshest. If one note or a segment of a melody feels unusual such as a change of mood, color or expression, or a particular harmony is striking, warm, or dark, it is a good idea to make note of it. Later on that freshness may get lost by repetitious practicing. One needs to keep them in mind and polish these SURPRISES at every practice session.

Once the general framework of a piece has been determined, the next step is to discern its form. From this perspective, one needs to break the work into smaller sections, i.e., A Section, B Section or Exposition and Development, etc. Then break it down to significant themes, motifs, transitions, closings, and other places of melodic and harmonic significance throughout the section. Finally, each phrase needs to be analyzed as to its mood, high point and inflection, etc. There is often a top melody along with a bass (and/or tenor) melody and its accompanying harmony in the middle register. The passage may not look at first glance to be two- or three-voiced in the accompaniment but it usually has many hidden voices besides the more prominent bass melody. Always look for moving voices. All of these lines must be studied separately for their individual expression, inflection and shading and put back together with great care, listening to the nuances and balance with the main melody and harmony. Since the harmonic progression is what holds the piece together, it is also advisable to block the harmonies and learn the inflection, direction and particularly the color or mood changes.

Each phrase may have one, two or three high points, depending on the length of the phrase. However, it must be very clear to the player as well as to the listener where the main climax falls, since the phrase leads to it (direction) and relaxes afterwards. Without this sense of forward motion, the listener cannot maintain a personal involvement in the piece. Bridge or transition passages must be played lightly, however beautifully, since they carry less musical importance.

There is no better time to begin the process of memorization than while the voices are separated and being analyzed in this manner. Study each detail as to the exact pattern, inflection and expression of each part, and memorize each little segment, phrase, etc., separately. Then combine them one by one carefully, listening especially to the beauty of the harmonies being created, their implications between the voices, the balance and the contrast in colors and characters.

This process reminds one of a jeweler making an art object--a crown, a necklace, a brooch, etc. He looks at <u>each</u> piece of precious stone and studies it from every angle to decide on the best way of cutting and polishing it. After every piece is ready for its particular setting, he assembles them according to the instructions. However, he has some freedom to select the right cut (emerald, faceted, pear-shaped, round, etc.). The arrangement of each stone, and the delicate and painstaking welding with platinum or gold also needs a great deal of hard, and sometimes tedious work, in completing a fine piece of jewelry.

The correct form should be maintained in each section and phrase of music, and every note must be in exact proportion to its size and importance. Frequently when one takes pieces apart to polish each phrase in detail, one loses the overall perspective of the piece. It is important that one always keeps in mind the entire piece in order to feel its overall flow and grand design. This may sound too structured and restricted. However, one can let go and be completely free in performance only after these preparations. Otherwise it may end up as a self-indulgent performance without a strong structure.

Memory

There are three kinds of memory:
1. Kinesthetic
2. Aural
3. Mental

Kinesthetic memory is when the performer relies on the physical memory, letting the fingers move. Aural memory depends entirely on one's ear and Mental memory is analyzing each detail and committing it to memory.

It is very easy to rely on the first two, as children do. However, they are not reliable under pressure unless one has an exceptionally keen ear. The mental memory is most dependable and desirable in performance, though it takes a great deal of work to acquire. The first procedure is the same as in learning a new piece.

1. Find the form (Sonata Allegro, Rondo, etc.) and divide into sections and then divide the sections into smaller units.

2. Find the pattern. When one finds the basic pattern in any elaborate passage, the whole passage becomes suddenly easier to play and to memorize. In the next example, the ascending pattern can be memorized as a C Major arpeggio with an inverted turn on each. Descending can be memorized as two notes (E and C) as the same C triad and V^9 or easier yet, as every other white key starting from the top E, embellished with an inverted trill and a turn, etc. Also, descending eighth notes form a C major scale down to D.

Example 7.1. Beethoven, Sonata, Op. 2, #3, 1st Movement.

One often finds layered lines. The top line (circled notes) in the example below continues to A#A an octave above to G#G etc., whereas the alto line (squared notes), F#F goes up an octave to E D#D C# etc.

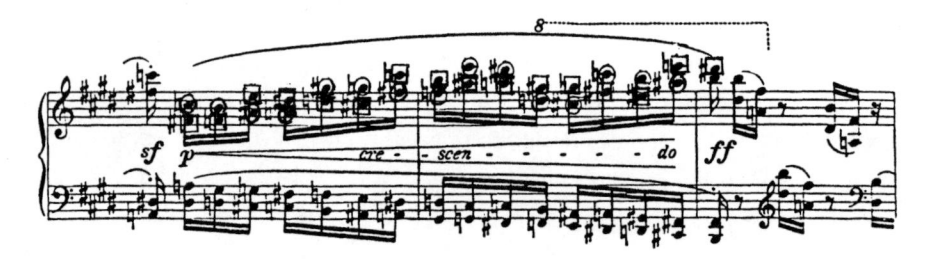

Example 7.2. Chopin, Etude, Op. 10, #3

In reality, both lines in the right hand are two descending chromatic lines as in the left hand only changing registers.

In the following passage from Beethoven's Opus 110, it is easy to see that the top notes are D^b Major scale. As to the patterns, this can easily be divided in two ways: (1) 2 (notes) + 3 + 3, and (2) 3 + 3 + 2.

Example 7.3. Beethoven, Op. 110, 2nd Movement.

Ravel's Jeux d'eau has a cadenza which is rather complicated. It reveals several patterns.

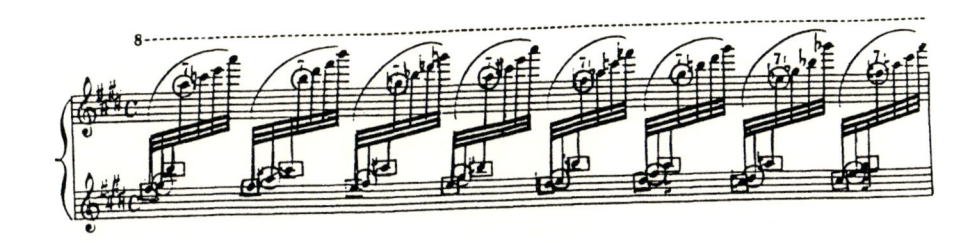

Example 7.4. Ravel, Jeux d'eau.

1. Right hand first note of each pattern is based on whole tone scale, only in zig-zag.
2. Right hand plays a major and a minor chord alternately.
3. Left hand bass line descends as whole tone scale.
4. The second notes of the left hand pattern are based on whole tone scale in zig-zag.
5. Left hand third notes (thumbs) descend as chromatic scale.

One may not need to know all these lines, but at least learn the bass and R.H. thumb line and the harmonic progression. Be able to start at any place using the correct fingerings, hands together, and each hand alone.

Always look for <u>patterns</u> to group several notes together. Never memorize note by note. This process can be compared to learning spelling. One looks at a word and remembers the shape at a glance. For instance "attention" has three t's sticking up. "Committee" has three double letters, etc. This is the pattern (or shape) one needs to look for. Finding common notes also helps.

Example 7.5. Beethoven, Sonata, Op. 7, 1st Movement.

In the above example (A), in the second measure, the top E^b in the right-hand chord and the left thumb on D^b are carried over to the left-hand pp chord. Then the left-hand chord (measure 4) leads into the right ff chord. The left thumb A^b (measure 4) changes to top A in the soprano in measure 5. The same pattern can be seen in measure 6. By eliminating the passing notes at (B), the passage becomes a broken F major triad. At (C) the left-hand downbeats and the fourth beats make up a descending C minor scale. The right-hand downbeats make a B minor triad and fourth beats a C minor triad for three measures. Throughout the passage, the last half of each measure consists of the same three notes (cross voicing), ascending in the right hand, descending in the left. There are also common notes (unison) on the second and fifth beats throughout the passage (marked by X's).

Contrapuntal pieces are harder to memorize. Learn each melodic line thoroughly and put them together harmonically. Know the form and divide it into small sections. It is not necessary for some pianists to go into such details, but it gives a lot of confidence to some others who may feel nervous in public.

Testing One's Memory

To test one's memory, the following suggestions are made:

1. Letter or number short sections (4 to 8 measures apart). Learn to play hands together and each hand alone.

2. Try playing one hand one measure, the other hand in the next, etc. In very slow pieces, even every half measure.

3. "Hopping." Using a partner, play along until the person says "hop." Stop playing physically but continue playing mentally with the hands on the lap. When the person says "hop" a second time, resume playing physically, continuing where one was playing mentally.

4. Be able to play the piece on a table top, a dummy keyboard, or hands crossed. An organ without the power can be used quite successfully.

5. Think through the entire piece away from the keyboard.

6. If time permits, write out the piece.

For some people, it is critical to know the fingerings thoroughly; for others it will not be necessary except in certain passages, e.g., fast runs or double 3rds, 4ths, etc. In these, know where the thumb falls or where the change of hand position occurs.

Even though one memorizes thoroughly one day, unless it is reviewed every day within the next few days, it may not be retained. After a few days, every other day will do and then once a week should be sufficient, but never stop reviewing until about one week before the performance. When one thinks of notes too close to the performance, it may hinder the spontaneity of music making during the performance.

Imagery

It is important to develop imagery early in one's study at the piano. Some composers such as Schumann and Debussy suggest the right mood of each piece by giving them appropriate titles which help us to project the proper images. However, imagery does not end with pieces such as these. Music is created from one's imagination, not from sound or patterns, in most cases. It is therefore important to think about what the music stands for or wants to express and to find the appropriate means to recreate the exact message.

Some pianists see imagery vividly right away while others feel the mood or the quality of the sound without a definite picture. Either approach is fine as long as each is clearly defined. To help young students develop these feelings, the teacher can suggest everyday expressions such as sadness, joy, humor, etc. They will begin to understand that when they see a "p" it means more than just soft. With the decreased volume there must be an expression of warmth, loneliness, or peace, for example. When they see "f," it may mean triumph, explosion of sheer joy or an intense passion, etc. According to each feeling, the tone quality will naturally vary. When this stage is reached, one begins to listen carefully to each note. Often without a wordy explanation on tone production, the appropriate sound comes out naturally. When this happens, the child is making music--a big leap from just playing notes. A young child can play "First Loss" (<u>Album for the Young</u>, Opus 68) by Schumann with beautifully sad feelings. The student should make up his own story, perhaps with some help from the teacher, so that he/she can produce a variety of sad tones--lonely, isolated, painful, etc. Suitable imagery can make a world of difference in learning.

In the more advanced repertoire, the opening of the Beethoven Sonata, Opus 31, No. 2, "Tempest" may suggest Heaven and Hell. Heaven will suggest peace, grandioso and serenity, and the scared, dark and uneasy agitato, for Hell, people scurrying about to escape. The opening of the Prelude from Franck's "Prelude, Choral and Fugue" may suggest a feeling of wonder, mysterious and uncertain, searching or longing for something never to be had. Choral can be an image of an old beautiful church, monks walking solemnly to receive communion in a deeply serene atmosphere. The intense feeling of pleading and inner struggle becomes more and more intense as the piece progresses, finally bursting in triumph. A sudden change of mood, color or dynamics (fp of subito p) needs a definite reason (a dark cloud suddenly lifting and the sun breaking through, etc.).

To develop one's imagination and understanding of great music, it is essential that one broaden and cultivate his mind by reading novels, appreciating art and listening to good music from an early age. We must remember that the essence of music is a combination of imagery and expression (message), taking shape in various sounds.

Preparation for Performing

There are two kinds of performers. The first perform as they like, using the pieces to satisfy their fancy and to show off. They are only concerned with the effect they create both technically and musically. The second group are true artists who respect the music and try to serve it by becoming the means to recreate the composer's intentions. The performer should not be aware of one's own presence, but rather become one with the music to make it come alive. Since pianists do not have the words to communicate as singers do, it is imperative to express enough in inflection, tone quality and nuances. Projection also needs to be emphasized so that the message will come across strongly to the listener.

During the performance, try to free oneself of any distractions or interfering thoughts. The best concentration happens when the mind is loose--not when trying hard. (For example, when reading an interesting book or watching a movie, one can get inside the story or characters and later be able to recall all of the details with ease.) If the mind is tense, however, it can block the flow of the music and also block the feeling. Fear is natural when performing but do not let it be disruptive. Simply acknowledge that it is there and ignore it. When paid attention to, the fear can grow stronger and disturb one's concentration.

One can never expect to play even halfway decently without good preparation. Six weeks before the performance, the whole program ought to be ready. This means that it is musically polished and memory and technique are very secure. It is also a good idea to practice fast passages or big skips faster than the tempo desired in performance. It makes one feel very comfortable to slow down to a tempo after this kind of practice. It is also helpful to play the whole piece through without warming up so that the weak spots become apparent. If one feels tension in some passages, it should be worked out. Learn how to release tension as soon as it starts to creep in by finding out what is causing it. This can often be done by dropping the shoulders, freeing the arm, raising the wrist or even taking a big breath. Eventually perform the whole program, imagining the performance situation.

The last six weeks are for playing for friends to shake off nerves and for final polishing. Securing the memory should be eased up to the week before the performance as mentioned earlier, then free the mind to feel completely spontaneous when performing. This can be done only after all of the preparation has been thoroughly done. Otherwise being spontaneous may become hazardous instead.

Finally, in performing, concentrate on listening from the first note, willing the fingertips to make <u>each</u> tone exactly as intended. Listening keenly makes one involved in music making. Even though something may not go as planned, think ahead. Never stop to think or analyze what was played. Always feel the forward motion of the rhythm. Project the mood, direction and expression so that the listeners will have a focus. Never hold back--there is no room for shyness or reservation when performing. Try to give 200% because it is only in this manner that one can ever attempt to convey the message and expression of the genius of the great composers.

Chapter 8

PEDAGOGY

Position at the Piano

A child should sit at the piano as he/she sits at the dinner table with a fork in one hand and a knife in the other. The elbows should be slightly out from the waist, comfortably hanging down from the shoulders, with the back straight. The feet should be on the floor or on a box, telephone books, etc., if the legs are not long enough for the feet to touch the floor. The child must not lean back on the bench. Only 1/3 to 1/2 of the bench should be occupied so that he/she is free to balance when necessary. It is imperative that the shoulders be down and relaxed. A child may start playing in the correct posture, but it is very easy for the shoulders to creep up. Therefore, the teacher must be <u>constantly</u> aware of the child's posture so that tension never develops in this area. If the shoulders are down, tension is not likely to develop in any other joints. The height of the bench must be adjusted so that the child's forearm is on the same horizontal plane as the keyboard.

Hand Position

One of the easiest ways to introduce a good hand position is for the child to make a light fist and place it on the keyboard. The fist should be gradually opened up into a five-finger position. The bridge should be the highest point. The first and second joints are curved and the wrist is held slightly lower than the bridge.

Figure 8.1. Basic hand position.

Make sure the thumb does not lie down but stands up on its tip so that it can operate as a finger with 2 joints. In other words, separate the thumb independently from the hand. When the hand is correctly placed on the keys, the fingertips should outline a semi-circle. (Please refer to Figure 3.2 in Chapter 3.) The thumb and little finger are placed close to the edge of the white keys, while the third finger is almost at the base of a black key.

Playing for the First Time

The first sounds the child produces at the keyboard should be the ones produced without any weight. It is easier to train the fingers on a tabletop at first. Students should learn to move the fingers up and down without involving the hand. For some reason, they never force on the table whereas they are apt to push down on the keys without releasing, feeling anxious to make the sound. When raised, the finger should stretch slightly at the 1st and 2nd joints to avoid any tension.

Figure 8.2. Correct Position

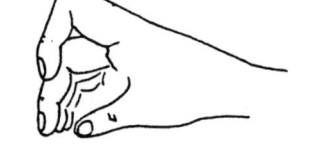

Figure 8.3. Incorrect Position

Though some people recommend that the fingers be more curved at the second joint as in Figure 8.3, there are two very good reasons why this is not a good position: (1) some tension is created at the bridge when the fingers are raised in this manner, and (2) in playing, the fingers drop as a unit rather than developing the first joint to control the speed of descent.

The child should be taught to produce a clear, light sound by going down to the tone spot and letting the key rebound right away. Do make sure that no tension remains by holding the key at the tone spot, never sticking at the bottom of the key.

Ideally, each sound made at the piano should have its own meaning or expression. When playing instruments such as the oboe, violin, or flute, the performer must intentionally prepare and produce each sound. This is also true for a singer. At the piano, this intentionality must be developed from the first note the child plays.

Unfortunately the majority of children are not taught to listen to the quality of the sound they produce, nor to express feeling at an early stage. Every sound, like a word, must be meaningful. Playing the piano must become as natural as speaking in one's native tongue. If the child is talked to only in a gentle manner at home, he learns only to speak nicely. The same goes with the tone quality produced on the piano.

Children normally have a keener ear than adults. Do make them listen to each note they play. If the child hears a beautiful tone, he/she is usually able to produce it without much explanation. He/she should be able to compare sounds that are beautiful, hard, dull, etc. Needless to say, the teacher should be able to produce any tone, including an imitation of what the child produced.

Ear Training

Daily training with a parent is most helpful at an early age. The best time to begin ear training with a child is said to be around age 3 or 4. If it is delayed until 6 or later, progress is much slower unless the child is born with an exceptional ear. By the time the child is 9, ear development becomes much slower. Children enjoy the ear training when enrolled in a class in which games and activities are employed as teaching tools. It is important to choose a well trained, creative teacher, who understands the child's rate of growth and development. Pushing too hard too fast may cause the child to give up in frustration, while going too slowly may leave the child bored.

Ear training can be taught using a variety of methods. Some are based on single notes, while others use chords as their starting point. There are good preparatory classes, but here are some exercises mothers can do at home.

A way to begin would be to have the child find a single note, e.g., D, all over the piano as quickly as possible. D is often used because it is easy for the child to find since it is between two black keys. (One could also choose any black key.) The child can play each D going up and down the piano, walking along the keyboard rather than stretching awkwardly from the bench. The mother can lead by playing a note in each octave in rhythm, having the child follow along playing the same note--the faster the better. Then add a note when ready. This exercise develops a quick reflex in the child. After a while the child can lead and let the mother play catch up. This game should be done in even rhythm, in dotted rhythms, as well as a variety of other ways. The mother must always be creative in approaching these activities.

After mastering several (or all) of the keys on the piano, a major third may be introduced in the same manner. A minor third may follow or even a major (or minor) second if the child likes the dissonance. (The child will participate more fully in these activities if allowed to choose the intervals, rhythms, etc. on a regular basis.) These are the first steps towards learning to transpose--a vitally important part of the ear training process.

Another approach is to use chord progressions for developing the ear. The mother will play a major triad and occasionally play a dominant triad in the first inversion. If the child is too young to say C, E, G, or B, D, G, he can choose an action to perform each time he hears a particular chord. For instance, he can stand up when he hears an I chord and sit on a chair with V. When the child can hear I, V, I easily, put in an IV chord in the second inversion (CFA). Again, assign a new motion to the chord such as raising the hands. When the key of C major has been mastered, move onto G, F and so on to cover all of the white keys. The order of the keys is not important. Rather, the recognition of relative pitch is the key to mastering ear training.

Also extremely important at this stage is the sense of rhythm which should be felt physically. Always clap in rhythm, hop, skip, dance together with the music.

Along with these activities, the child should be allowed to sing easy tunes, such as folk songs. It would be wonderful if these can be sung with as much feeling and musicality as possible from the start. For some children singing in pitch is difficult. If they can recognize the pitch by hearing, it will not be too necessary to correct the pitch in singing all the time. That will later develop on its own.

The child does not need to start playing the piano right away since his hands are usually too small and his fingers too weak until approximately age 5. However, he should be encouraged to play simple tunes finding notes and harmonies on his own. Encourage him to experiment at the piano as much as possible. All experimenting should be done musically-- expressing a mood and always with beautiful tone. If a harsh sound is accidentally played, it should be pointed out and corrected immediately.

Transposition

As soon as the child is able to play a short tune, transposition should be introduced. The child does not need to read the music, rather he should depend on the ear to play a tune in a few easy keys at every lesson.

The following exercise is excellent for young students as well as adults. First do them without the harmonies, each hand separately then both hands together, and later as written.

Example 8.1. Five-finger exercise

Reading

Reading can be developed by teaching several notes at each lesson. If a child has difficulty in learning the notes, let him dictate writing big notes on a staff. One could use red for space notes, blue for line notes and one day write whole notes and another day half-notes, etc. If one can write, one can read.

For the first few months, it is permissible for a child to read each hand separately before putting them together. However, the child should be able to read both hands together at a slow tempo before too long. Always point out and have the child find patterns in the music so that he/she learns to read groups of notes, but never single notes. It would be ideal to be so careful as not to make any mistake in note reading, rhythm and fingering. Encourage the child to play slowly enough to avoid making mistakes.

First Lessons and Practicing

At an early stage of development, it would be good to have two weekly lessons to insure that the child fully understands and can demonstrate the concepts taught at the previous lesson. If any errors are made, it is much easier to correct them if they have been practiced for just a day or two rather than for an entire week.

In order for lessons to be beneficial, there must be clear lines of communication between the teacher and the student. The teacher must encourage students, however young, to be creative, but at the same time, the teacher must also be able to show the various possibilities in order to make the piece more beautiful and exciting. One can never teach what one cannot do.

The first several lessons are very important for the child and the teacher. During this time, the teacher must explain and practice together with the child. The child must have no doubts as to what to do and what is expected of him/her at each practice session. Things that must be covered are slow sectional playing with no mistakes, listening carefully to each note and its tone quality, accurate rhythm, and counting aloud. If a mistake is made, the child must stop immediately and go back a measure or two to the beginning of the phrase. The second time the passage should be played correctly and repeated perfectly at least a few times before moving on. (If the mistake is not corrected in this manner, the child is learning to practice making mistakes.) This process is painstaking, but it really pays off. When a child has learned to be careful in slow practicing, pick up the tempo gradually. Practicing too long at a slow tempo can make progress slower than necessary.

At the very beginning, it is almost a necessity to have parent support for practicing at home. The adult does not need to be trained in music, but needs to be interested in what the child is doing. It is important to schedule a regular practice time for the child and make sure it is adhered to. Whoever sits with the child should not supervise practicing unless the child demonstrates that his mind is wandering. Rather than interfering, the parent needs to gently coax the child to pay more attention. Most children need to know that a parent cares and is listening. Part of the practice session can be listening to a tape of the previous lesson (taping the lessons is very valuable) to make sure the child knows what has been assigned and what to correct and to improve.

Challenging Students

A common fault among teachers is that they make the lessons too easy. They do not challenge the students enough. Countless freshmen entering music schools have complained that they did not have the support they needed or were not pushed hard enough in the early years, especially technically. It takes three times longer to develop one's technique at age 18 than at age 10 or 12. For this reason, with very musical students, a great deal of technique should be developed as early as possible. These students must be aware that the exercises are the tools they will utilize in the future. However, the needs of less gifted students are somewhat different. They should be able to sight read well and enjoy playing music. Exactness and perfection can be modified to a degree so that they enjoy making music. They may also learn what to listen for in music.

It seems to work best to develop one's technique covering the wide range of the keyboard by playing big pieces like Mendelssohn's Rondo Cappricio, Chopin's Scherzi, Liszt's Etudes at a fairly young age (12 - 15). Students seem to enjoy bravura passages: fast octaves, runs, and skips. Unless virtuosity is developed early, the hand may not form well and develop the flexibility to meet the tremendous demand of highly technical pieces later.

Chapter 9

PIANISTIC ANALYSIS

Chopin Nocturne

Here are a few compositions to summarize various points discussed in the previous chapters: Chopin for analyzing the melodic line, Debussy for pedaling and Ravel for coloring. Of course, there are numerous ways of interpreting a piece pianistically. One does not always play a piece the same way twice. There should be as many kinds of interpretation as there are players. However here is a Chopin Nocturne as our first example to show how a melody in Romantic music can be conceived as to its inflection, tonal changes and direction. The high point of each phrase is indicated with arrow signs.

Example 9.1. Chopin, Nocturne, Op. 15, #2.

The first two upbeats seem as though they are leading into a melancholy, intimate confession.

Measure 1. These upbeats lead into the three notes, A#, G#, E#, to be sung with a subtle rubato and diminuendo, with emphasis on the downbeat A#, then two light C#s. A little delayed final C# since this serves as upbeat to the next expressive downbeat C#. This is to avoid the monotony repeated notes often create. Re-phrasing is a solution to this problem.

Measure 2. After clinging to the downbeat long enough, slur off to C# on the second beat as questioning. The next two notes (A# and B) might be as mellow as the opening notes but with a little more assertion for what is to come.

Measure 3. With more rubato and more emphasis on the downbeat A#, sing down this time with crescendo to a rich E# and D, taking time on these two important notes and lighten up on the next two C#s. Again the last C# is an upbeat to the next downbeat C#.

Measure 4. The downbeat C# calls for a deeper tone and slurs off on 32nds. The last three notes can be played almost as subito p with the utmost delicacy or crescendo leading into the next phrase. The next two upbeats should sound quite differently with much more assertion and eagerness.

Measure 5. Again with some rubato on the downbeat, sing to F##, taking enough time to emphasize it and move onto two D#s, especially making a rich nuance on the second beat with left-hand harmony. The last D# leads to the next measure with much crescendo.

Measure 6. Here the strong downbeat D# to high F#, the skip of a 10th, carries a very intense expression (high point of the eight-measure phrase), a feeling of longing or desperate pleading. Take plenty of time, as a singer would, to sing up, being careful to match the tone in volume as well as in tone quality. Using the hand weight on both notes will result in a rich tone without harshness. After holding long enough the tied F# with the feeling of crescendo, slur off on D#. Much more relaxed gentle upbeats (F# and G#) lead to the next A# with a swing. The harmony in the left hand supports the rich melody by the use of inverted slurs moving towards the beat.

Measure 7. Downbeat A# dances up and leads gracefully to G# with the trill which should tremble with a touch of excitement, perhaps of momentary happiness. (This can also express great sadness.) The trill must be very light with a slight crescendo in the middle and diminuendo at the end. Feel a fermata on the rest and play the last G# almost as a grace note to the next downbeat F#. The colorful three-voiced harmony in the left hand should not be neglected, especially in the middle voice legato from F# to E#. The tenor melody also compliments the top melody.

Measure 8. All of a sudden the instant hope disappears to a darker downbeat VI chord. Then an even darker and richer secondary dominant. Take sufficient time to resolve on V, nuancing each harmonic change before returning to the theme. Keep at least four measures (or eight measures in faster pieces) as a phrase to hold it together. It becomes annoying and loses direction when phrases become fragmented, though the expression may change a few times within a measure.

Debussy Pedaling

Generally, French Impressionistic music can take longer pedals because it is often based on the pentatonic or whole-tone scales or modes which do not have half steps. In pieces such as "La Cathédrale engloutie," there are many places where long pedaling should be taken (refer to Chapter 2, p. 18). In the same piece, one finds that three-measure pedaling is most suitable. Debussy's music has many different colors which need to be layered but not blurred.

Example 9.2. Debussy, "La Cathédrale engloutie"

In delicate pieces like "La Fille aux Cheveux de Lin," all pedaling is somewhat like 1/2 damping to avoid thick sound except when the low bass notes are to be held through. Here a great deal of overlapping pedal as well as 1/2 pedal is employed. Even for complete clearance, a slight overlapping pedal will blend the harmonies more beautifully for a dreamy effect. At A, in order to play the inner harmony on time, the bass note G^b and soprano G^b are to be caught in a clean pedal a second before the downbeat. It needs a quick shift of the left hand to make the harmony sound undisturbed by the leap.

At B, the same treatment is done, except the right hand A^b is to be held over to insure the legato melody. A^b should be caught in the pedal taken on grace note C^b in the bass an instant before the downbeat. Since A^b is in p level in the high register, it is not disturbing. This is a better choice than having to break the melody line with a clear pedal on the low C^b.

C indicates all 1/2 pedaling overlapped for a dreamy effect.

At D, 1/2 pedals are optional. A 1/2 damping pedal may work just as nicely, depending on the piano. It is needless to point out that the tone here varies from gentle and mellow melody to melting harmonious sound, both requiring a brushing touch of various speed and depth.

Example 9.3. Debussy, "La Fille aux Chaveaux de Lin"

Example 9. 3. Debussy, "La Fille aux Chaveaux de Lin" (cont'd)

Ravel's Coloring

Ravel is extraordinarily colorful, elegant and sophisticated. While Debussy requires layering of pastel colors, Ravel chooses to glitter. Since the tone needs to sparkle without heaviness, the quick use of the fingertip action, the nail-under touch, is most appropriate to create lightness and clarity. Most of Ravel's typical colors come from the dissonance of the seconds, especially the half steps. The seconds (7th or 9ths) can sound ugly, if played equally loud or heavily. However, when one of them is colored and the other extremely soft, a unique glitter results. One needs to analyze and listen to determine which note of the seconds to favor. When the seconds are written as wide intervals as 7th or 9th, both notes can be colored successfully if they are in the higher register.

Example 9.4. Ravel, "Jeux d'eau."

In the above example, half steps are marked in circles and whole steps enclosed in squares. There are more seconds within each hand which are not marked (in order to avoid clutter). Since the right hand has the melody, the opening needs the color on the top D#, keeping the bass E quiet. The downbeat should have no accent but a sense of flowing. Listen to the beautiful harmonization between the left hand B and D#. The most expressive part of the melody is D# F# D#. Sing them with care (tres doux). Because the second half of the second and fourth beats (32nd notes) serve as upbeats, use the lightest touch for delicate pp leading into the next beats. (There are twice as many notes to play and they all need to be at least twice as soft--they are only bridges.) Rephrasing from the second G# as shown with a slur to the fourth beat D# will not only keep them light but lead to the next beat smoothly.

Measure 3 calls for the same care, only brighter. Rolled harmonies are added against the 32nd notes, giving a sudden dark shading. If not careful, they can sound too heavy. Measure 4 is the transition, shifting to softer and more mysterious on each half beat. At measure 5, since the register moves down, it is very important to keep the harmonies soft except to bring out the tenor G#, new color, keeping the B^b sixth below light enough in order to avoid colliding with the right-hand C. On the second half of the 2nd and 4th beats, Ravel not only has the four 32nds but the half steps (right-hand E# and G) to play together. G is much more important, acting as a resolution from the tenser G#. One can learn to place the thumb as an Organ Thumb, so that G will dominate over E# though only in p level. In measure 6, the repeated G# tenor eventually leads to the more definite melodic line. A very subtle crescendo in the preceding G#s and a slight hesitation before the final G# for emphasis (without an accent) is in order before the descending diminuendo. The last half of the measure again calls for a delicate tone in the right hand. Here two sets of whole tone scales are used. The second scale needs to be as light as a delicate piece of lace, disappearing into the grace notes of the return of the melody.

As mentioned before, it is extremely important to lighten the texture in the lower register when seconds are involved as in the next example. Since the left-hand A# is to be colored, the right-hand B ought to be ppp to avoid a muddy sound.

Example 9.5, Ravel, "Jeux d'eau."

INDEX

A. Accent, 84
Alberti bass, 75
Analysis, 114
Arpeggio, 30

B. Balancing, 39
Bebung, 67

C. Cadenzas, 66
Chords
    arpeggio, 30
    blocking, 75
    broken, 30
    first, 43
    pp, 42
    rolled, 76-78
    staccato, 37
    third, 84
Coloring, 69
Con anima, 87
Crescendo, 23, 79

D. Diminuendo, 23, 79

E. Ear training, 109-111
Exercises, 89
    joints, 94
    key release, 95-96
    stretching, 89-92
    thumbs, 92, 93

F. Fingering, 47-52
Forte, 83

G. Glissando, 46
Grace notes, 63

H. Hands, 26, 36, 50, 107, 108
Harmony, 53, 73
Hemiola, 80

I. Imagery, 97, 103, 104

K. Keybed, 3

L. Learning, 97
Legato, 9, 10
Lessons, 112

M. Melody, 53
    regrouping, 53
    repeated notes, 61
    treatment of, 56
Memory, 97, 103

N. Notes
    grace, 63
    high, 58
    inner, 84
    long, 57
    repeated, 36
    tied, 60

O. Octaves, 39-41
Ornaments, 62

P. Pedagogy, 107
Pedal, pedaling, 12, 14, 15
    crescendo, 23
    damper, 13
    Debussy, 116-119
    diminuendo, 23
    finger, 21
    fluttering, 21-22
    half, 17
    half-damping, 19-20
    overlapping, 16
    shaking, 21
    sostenuto, 12
    staccato, 24
    sustaining, 16
    syncopated, 16
    trill, 21
    una corda, 12
    uses of, 16-24
Performing, 97, 104-106
Pianistic analysis, 114
Piano, 83

Playing, 10, 27, 41-45, 50-51, 58, 79, 85, 108
Practicing, 28, 85, 88, 112

R. Rallentando, 87
Ravel, 120-122
Reading, 111

Rests, 81
Rhythm, 82
Ritardando, 87
Ritenuto, 87
Rubato, 86

S. Scales, 27-30
Sforzando, 84
Shoulders, 39
Skips, 38
Slurs, 66-69
Sostenuto, 87
Staccato, 10
Syncopation, 64

T. Technique, 26
   arpeggio, 30
   balancing, 39
   broken chords, 30
   connection, 46
   crossed hands, 50
   different notes, 45
   doorknob rotation, 37
   double notes, 35
   double trill, 33
   false trill, 34
   fast repeated notes, 36
   fingering, 47
   first chords, 43
   flat finger tips, 43
   glissando, 46
   hand, 26
   karate chop, 43
   octaves, 39
   organ thumb, 42
   playing *f* and *p*, 41
   playing *ff* in bass, 43
   playing *pp* chords, 42
   practicing, 28, 85, 88, 112
   rotation, 26, 27
   shoulder, 39
   skips, 38
   staccato chords, 37
   switching, 51
   transfer, 47
   trill, 32-34
   turn 31, 32
   white notes between black keys, 44
Thumbs, 42, 75, 92, 93
Timing, 84
Tone, 1, 84
   bell-like, 6
   bright, 8
   chordal, 6
   colorless, 3
   double legato, 10
   harmonious, 3
   production, 1, 10, 11
   quality, 3
   singing, 5
   spot, 1
   staccato, 10
   vibration, 8
   weight, 5, 9
Transposition, 111
Tremolo, 86-87
Triplets, 33, 64-65
Turns, 62

V. Voicing, 69

NOTES